THE AMERICAN SONGBOOK

Tempo
A Rowman & Littlefield Music Series on Rock, Pop, and Culture

Series Editor: Scott Calhoun

Tempo: A Rowman & Littlefield Music Series on Rock, Pop, and Culture offers titles that explore rock and popular music through the lens of social and cultural history, revealing the dynamic relationship between musicians, music, and their milieu. Like other major art forms, rock and pop music comment on their cultural, political, and even economic situation, reflecting the technological advances, psychological concerns, religious feelings, and artistic trends of their times. Contributions to the **Tempo** series are the ideal introduction to major pop and rock artists and genres.

The American Songbook: Music for the Masses, by Ann van der Merwe
Bob Dylan: American Troubadour, by Donald Brown
Bon Jovi: America's Ultimate Band, by Margaret Olson
British Invasion: The Crosscurrents of Musical Influence, by Simon Philo
Bruce Springsteen: American Poet and Prophet, by Donald L. Deardorff II
The Clash: The Only Band That Mattered, by Sean Egan
Kris Kristofferson: Country Highwayman, by Mary G. Hurd
Patti Smith: America's Punk Rock Rhapsodist, by Eric Wendell
Paul Simon: An American Tune, by Cornel Bonca
Ska: The Rhythm of Liberation, by Heather Augustyn
Sting and The Police: Walking in Their Footsteps, by Aaron J. West
Warren Zevon: Desperado of Los Angeles, by George Plasketes

THE AMERICAN SONGBOOK

Music for the Masses

Ann van der Merwe

ROWMAN & LITTLEFIELD
Lanham • Boulder • New York • London

Published by Rowman & Littlefield
A wholly owned subsidary of The Rowman & Littlefield Publishing Group, Inc.
4501 Forbes Boulevard, Suite 200, Lanham, Maryland 20706
www.rowman.com

Unit A, Whitacre Mews, 26-34 Stannary Street, London SE11 4AB

British Library Cataloguing in Publication Information Available

Library of Congress Cataloging-in-Publication Data

Names: Van der Merwe, Ann Ommen, 1978– author.
Title: The American songbook : music for the masses / Ann van der Merwe.
Description: Lanham, MD : Rowman & Littlefield, 2017. | Series: Tempo : a Rowman & Littlefield music series on rock, pop, and culture | Includes bibliographical references and index.
Identifiers: LCCN 2016022207 (print) | LCCN 2016023727 (ebook) | ISBN 9781442242449 (cloth : alk. paper) | ISBN 9781442242456 (electronic)
Subjects: LCSH: Popular music—United States—History and criticism.
Classification: LCC ML3477 .V36 2017 (print) | LCC ML3477 (ebook) | DDC 782.421640973—dc23 LC record available at https://lccn.loc.gov/2016022207

∞ ™ The paper used in this publication meets the minimum requirements of American National Standard for Information Sciences Permanence of Paper for Printed Library Materials, ANSI/NISO Z39.48-1992.

Printed in the United States of America

To Liezel and Ewan
I hope you will come to know and love these songs as
much as I do

CONTENTS

Series Editor's Foreword   ix
Timeline   xi
Acknowledgments   xix
Introduction   xxi

1 Essentials of the American Songbook   1
2 Authors of the American Songbook   13
3 The American Songbook on Stage   27
4 The American Songbook on Screen   39
5 Jazz and the American Songbook   51
6 Interpreters of the American Songbook   63
7 The American Songbook in the 1950s and 1960s   83
8 The American Songbook Today   95

Epilogue: Amateurs and the American Songbook   115
Further Reading   117
Further Listening   121
Index   129
About the Author   133

SERIES EDITOR'S FOREWORD

Opening up the American Songbook begins an interactive experience with popular song standards that resist stagnation by their very virtue of being a part of a continuing performing arts project. The songs appeal, quite simply, to new generations of performers and audiences. They are durable, reliable moments for showcasing talent and telling nuanced stories that have the power to bring listeners into a longer, larger American narrative. I find in them a pleasure in their familiarity and frequently confident, optimistic statements of selfhood, as much as I hear in them a reminder of the tensions with which the threads of individual talents are woven into the fabric of society.

Ann van der Merwe tells the lively story of the development of the songbook and its role in shaping many of our most memorable cultural moments on stage and screen. As she looks closely at how songs became popular American standards and how composers have either been acclaimed for or eclipsed by their songs' popularity, she's able to examine the complicated, often contested, notions of originality and ownership, showing us that the essential American offer of opportunity always comes with strings attached. The very notion of a song becoming a standard, meaning that not only are performers attracted to it but audiences could expect an artist to be able to perform it and perform it well because of the essential skills the song requires, speaks to other threads tensely woven through American history: faith in amateurism and the privileging of the professional. Some songs are written for masses and then eventually distributed to the masses. Some songs are easy to sing

well but harder to sing exceptionally well. When a performance becomes exceptional and is widely heard, some songs then take on the
qualities of that singular moment of artistry in a permanent way. And
yet, the American Songbook contains all these instances and stories
without becoming a memorial to *e pluribus unum*. In it still are plenty
of opportunities to participate in and continue to add to a growing,
unified chorus. From Irving Berlin to Michael Bublé, from Cole Porter,
Duke Ellington, and George and Ira Gershwin, to Tony Bennett, Harry
Connick Jr., Audra McDonald, and dozens more, when the tune hits us
with each new performance, there is enough potency in the song itself
to lift us and knit us into a larger community as there is a chance for this
to be the defining moment of all time.

Scott Calhoun

TIMELINE

Cultural Events

1877: Thomas Edison invents the phonograph

1881: Czar Nicholas of Russia is assassinated; persecution of Jews follows

1884: Mark Twain publishes *The Adventures of Huckleberry Finn*

1890: Yosemite is designated a National Park

1892: Columbian Exposition (Chicago)
1892: Ellis Island opens as an immigrant processing center

Events in the Development of the American Songbook

1885: Jerome Kern is born
1888: Irving Berlin is born

1891: Cole Porter is born

1895: Oscar Hammerstein II and Lorenz Hart are born

1896: Ira Gershwin is born

1898: George Gershwin is born

1899: Fred Astaire and Duke Ellington are born

1902: Richard Rodgers is born

1903: Orville and Wilbur Wright make their historic first flight
1903: *The Great Train Robbery* is shown in American movie theaters

1903: Vernon Duke is born

1905: Harold Arlen is born

1906: First AM radio program broadcast

1907: The Ziegfeld Follies is produced for the first time

1908: Henry Ford invents the Model-T

1908: Ethel Merman is born

1909: NAACP is established

1909: Johnny Mercer is born

1910: Django Reinhardt is born

1911: Irving Berlin writes "Alexander's Ragtime Band"

1912: *Titanic* sinks on its maiden voyage

1914: World War I begins
1914: ASCAP (American Society of Composers, Arrangers, and Publishers) is founded

1914: Jerome Kern writes "They Didn't Believe Me"

1915: *Lusitania* is sunk, pushing the United States closer to war

1915: Princess Theater presents Jerome Kern's *Nobody Home*
1915: Frank Sinatra and Billie Holiday are born

1917: United States enters World War I

1917: Ella Fitzgerald and Helen Forrest are born

1918: World War I ends

1920: Prohibition Act becomes law, making alcohol consumption illegal

1920: Jerome Kern's "Look for the Silver Lining" is featured in *Sally*

1922: George and Ira Gershwin publish "I'll Build a Stairway to Paradise"
1922: Judy Garland is born

1924: Isham Jones and Gus Kahn write "It Had to Be You"
1924: Fred Astaire stars in *Lady, Be Good* (George and Ira Gershwin) on Broadway

1925: F. Scott Fitzgerald publishes *The Great Gatsby*
1925: *The Grand Ole Opry* radio show premieres

1926: Irving Berlin writes "Blue Skies"
1926: Tony Bennett and Carolyn Leigh are born

1927: Charles Lindbergh flies from New York to Paris

1927: Florenz Ziegfeld presents *Showboat*
1927: *The Jazz Singer* is released, featuring Irving Berlin's "Blue Skies"

1928: Walt Disney creates Mickey Mouse

1929: Wall Street Crash marks the beginning of the Great Depression
1929: The Academy of Motion Picture Arts and Sciences gives its first awards

1929: Mitchell Parish adds lyrics to Hoagy Carmichael's "Stardust"
1929: Cy Coleman is born

1930: Ethel Merman stars in *Girl Crazy* on Broadway (George and Ira Gershwin)
1930: Stephen Sondheim is born

1931: Duke Ellington publishes "It Don't Mean a Thing If It Ain't Got That Swing"

1932: Amelia Earhart flies across the Atlantic

1932: Cole Porter writes "Night and Day"

1933: Prohibition ends

1933: Busby Berkeley produces the film *42nd Street*
1933: "Easter Parade" is performed in *As Thousands Cheer* (Irving Berlin) on Broadway

1934: Ethel Merman stars in *Anything Goes* (Cole Porter) on Broadway

1935: Fred Astaire sings "Cheek to Cheek" and "Isn't It a Lovely Day" in *Top Hat*

1936: Fred Astaire sings "The Way You Look Tonight" in *Swing Time*

1937: George Gershwin dies

1938: *Snow White and The Seven Dwarfs* is released, the first feature-length animated film

1939: World War II begins

1939: Coleman Hawkins records his iconic version of "Body and Soul"
1939: *The Wizard of Oz* starring Judy Garland is released

1940: Billie Holiday records "Body and Soul" for the first time

1941: United States enters WWII
after the Japanese attack on Pearl
Harbor

1942: Irving Berlin writes "White
Christmas"

1943: *Oklahoma!* (Rodgers and
Hammerstein) premieres on
Broadway
1943: Lorenz Hart dies

1945: World War II ends

1945: Jerome Kern dies

1946: Frank Sinatra records his
first album, *The Voice of Frank
Sinatra*
1946: Ethel Merman stars in
Annie Get Your Gun (Irving
Berlin) on Broadway

1948: Columbia Records
introduces the LP (long playing
record)

1948: Judy Garland and Fred
Astaire star on screen in *Easter
Parade*

1949: George Orwell publishes
1984

1950: Korean War begins

1951: *An American in Paris*
showcases the songs of George
and Ira Gershwin

1952: *Singin' in the Rain*
showcases the songs of Nacio
Herb Brown and Arthur Freed

1953: Armistice in Korea

1953: Elvis Presley makes his first
recording with Sun Records
1953: Django Reinhardt dies

1954: Judy Garland sings "The
Man That Got Away" in *A Star Is
Born*

1954: Bill Haley's recording of "Rock Around the Clock" becomes a national hit

1956: Ella Fitzgerald records her first two songbook collections (Porter/Rodgers and Hart)

1957: Russia launches Sputnik

1957: *West Side Story* (Leonard Bernstein/Stephen Sondheim) premieres on Broadway
1957: Billie Holiday releases the album *Body and Soul*
1957: Brian Stokes Mitchell is born

1958: Billie Holiday releases *Lady in Satin*

1959: Cy Coleman and Carolyn Leigh write "The Best Is Yet to Come"
1959: Billie Holiday dies

1960: Oscar Hammerstein II dies

1961: Vietnam War begins

1961: Johnny Mercer and Henry Mancini write "Moon River"

1962: Walmart is founded

1962: Duke Ellington and Stephane Grappelli collaborate on their "Jazz Violin Session"

1964: Civil Rights Act of 1964

1964: Ella Fitzgerald records her final songbook collection (Johnny Mercer)
1964: Cole Porter dies
1964: Diana Krall is born

1966: *Cabaret* (John Kander and Fred Ebb) premieres on Broadway

1967: The Beatles release *Sgt. Pepper's Lonely Hearts Club Band*
1967: Harry Connick Jr. is born

1968: Martin Luther King Jr. is assassinated

1969: Neil Armstrong walks on the moon

1969: Judy Garland dies

1970: Apollo 13 mission

1970: *Company* (Stephen Sondheim) premieres on Broadway
1970: Audra MacDonald is born

1971: Starbucks is founded

1974: Duke Ellington dies

1975: Michael Bublé is born

1976: The Apple computer company is founded

1976: Johnny Mercer dies

1979: Richard Rodgers dies

1981: MTV premieres

1982: First compact discs are sold

1983: Carolyn Leigh and Ira Gershwin die

1984: Ethel Merman dies

1986: Space shuttle *Challenger* accident

1986: Harold Arlen dies

1987: Fred Astaire dies

1989: Irving Berlin dies
1989: Harry Connick Jr. performs on the soundtrack to *When Harry Met Sally*

1990: Invention of the World Wide Web
1990: Hubble Space Telescope launched

1993: Diana Krall releases her first album, *Stepping Out*

1996: Ella Fitzgerald dies

1997: "The Way You Look Tonight" is featured in *My Best Friend's Wedding*

1998: Frank Sinatra dies

1999: Helen Forrest dies

2001: September 11 terrorist attacks in New York City and Washington, D.C.

2003: Space shuttle *Columbia* disaster

2003: Michael Bublé records his first album, *Michael Bublé*

2004: Cy Coleman dies

2006: Tony Bennett records *Duets: An American Classic*

2007: Michael Bublé releases *Call Me Irresponsible*

2008: "It Only Takes a Moment" (Jerry Herman) is featured in *WALL-E*

2009: Harry Connick Jr. releases *Your Songs*; Diana Krall releases *Quiet Nights*

2010: Apple releases the iPad

2011: Tony Bennett records *Duets II*

2014: Tony Bennett and Lady Gaga collaborate on *Cheek to Cheek*

2015: Tony Bennett releases *The Silver Lining* with pianist Bill Charlap

ACKNOWLEDGMENTS

Every book is made possible by people who help the author, and this one is no exception. In this case, my debts are largely personal—which makes them especially wonderful to share with my readers.

First, I am deeply grateful to Scott Calhoun. In addition to providing editorial feedback throughout my writing process, he also led me to this topic in the first place. After my initial proposal, he continued to exchange ideas with me until we developed a plan that centered on the American Songbook. As such, he has been an influential presence from beginning to end, and I am thankful for his thoughtfulness, his creativity, and his confidence in me—all of which have made this book possible. Of course, I am also grateful to those members of the Rowman & Littlefield family who have played a special role in bringing my manuscript into print, namely Natalie Mandziuk, Bennett Graff, and Monica Savaglia. It has been a great pleasure to work with this publisher for a second time, and I am honored to be among its list of authors.

The many men and women who have studied and written about this repertoire have informed my own work in countless ways. Among those who have proven most influential are Gerald Bordman, Philip Furia, Edward Jablonski, Jeffrey Magee, Howard Pollack, Benjamin Sears, and Alec Wilder. Their enthusiasm for these songs matches my own, and I am grateful for the many ways in which they have shaped my connection to and knowledge of these songs.

As someone who first came to know these songs by singing them, I also owe a debt of gratitude to those who introduced them to me as a repertoire and nurtured my interest in performing them. These include Kari Jones, my first voice teacher; Barrington Coleman, who taught me during my college years and with whom I sang many Gershwin and Porter tunes; and the amazing Marni Nixon, who worked with me during one of her master classes and whose suggestion that this repertoire was "where I lived" will always stick with me.

Of course, without the support of my family and friends, I would not have had the time or resources needed to write anything at all. My husband has—as we like to say in our household—"carried the team" on numerous occasions. My children have entertained themselves at times when they would rather have had me read to them than write my own words. And even their interruptions have inspired me in the long run. My parents also continue to be a great support to me, offering encouragement and help in any way they can. In addition to all of this, I have a wonderful circle of friends and colleagues who make a difference simply by believing in me.

Lastly, and most importantly, I am grateful to God for giving me the wonderful gift of music, the ability to write about it, and the desire to share my passion for it with others. He is the source of everything, and I am both privileged and humbled to do His work.

INTRODUCTION

On 11 February 2003, record producer David Foster released a new album by a then relatively unknown Canadian singer named Michael Bublé. Entitled simply *Michael Bublé*, the album proved to be a success, introducing a new voice to millions of listeners around the globe—and reintroducing them to songs of previous decades. Some, like Van Morrison's "Moondance" and Freddie Mercury's "Crazy Little Thing Called Love," could be considered cover versions of modern classics—Bublé's reinterpretations of the original recordings from the 1970s. Others, though, took listeners back even further into the twentieth century—to a time when "cover version" was not even part of the music industry vocabulary because most songs were recorded by multiple artists soon after they were written. "The Way You Look Tonight," for instance, was introduced by Fred Astaire in the 1936 film *Swing Time*, but recordings of the song by Bing Crosby and Billie Holliday were also released that same year. Numerous other renditions from subsequent years have become familiar, including those from Ella Fitzgerald, Tony Bennett, and Frank Sinatra. As such, Bublé's version of the song is a continuation of this earlier practice in popular music—one in which the song has a life of its own, apart from any specific performer or performance. It is songs like these—songs also commonly known as standards because they constituted a common or "standard" repertoire of popular music for singers in the early twentieth century—that make up the American Songbook.

In 2006, Tony Bennett partnered with a long list of celebrated pop stars to produce another album that combines some of these standards from the American Songbook along with a few modern classics. Called *Duets: An American Classic*, this album presents all of its songs as music for any type of singer—not just a repertoire for singers of a certain vocal style that dates back to the early twentieth century. To make this point, Bennett purposely chose a wide range of collaborators *and* material, all rendered in fresh ways by a variety of voices. Just five years later, Bennett extended his project with *Duets II*. This time, he involved more youthful performers—ones who would not only expand the stylistic range of the earlier album but also target the youngest listeners in American popular music.

At first glance, albums like these might seem like revivals—attempts to revisit the musical past. In reality, though, they have accomplished something very different. After all, the American Songbook has hardly been absent from popular culture since the 1950s. These songs have enjoyed a continual presence through rereleases of original recordings and films of the period, in contemporary performances by both Broadway and jazz artists, and in more casual renditions heard at weddings and other celebrations. To give but one example, consider the widespread familiarity of "The Way You Look Tonight." Many people of all ages and backgrounds have heard some version of this song, and they recognize it when they hear it. Despite this continued presence, however, these songs have not been at the forefront of popular music as they once were. What Bublé and Bennett have done is try to bring this music back to the masses, and they have been fairly successful in their efforts. Music that has been the domain of mostly older listeners and fans of musical theater and jazz for the past few decades is now becoming familiar to a much wider range of people.

Yet in its own time, the American Songbook enjoyed this kind of popularity—perhaps even a broader type of popularity than can be achieved today. It was familiar not just to one or two demographic groups but to an overwhelming majority of the American public—not to mention a significant international audience. It was music written with broad applicability and broad appeal in mind, music to be used and heard in a wide variety of circumstances. It was music on universal themes such as love and loss, music capable of speaking to and reaching the heart of almost anyone—regardless of age or background. It was music for the masses in the biggest sense, music that nearly everyone knew and many loved. And it happened because of the unique cultural climate in which it was created.

CREATING AN AMERICAN MUSICAL IDENTITY

At the beginning of the twentieth century's second decade, the world was on the brink of the First World War—a war that would prove devastating on almost every level, from the sheer number of casualties and immense geographic destruction to the long-term political ramifications that would lead to another war twenty-five years later. Yet before the war began, the United States was among the few countries wary of the conflict—a sentiment that kept it out of the war for almost three years. Much of Europe, on the other hand, seemed to welcome the war, at least as a concept. Many thought it would be a short and decisive series of battles that would clear the international atmosphere and distinguish the global powers from the lesser nations. Of course, the reality was a disastrously long and largely unresolved series of conflicts that would only muddy the waters of international politics and leave millions around the world with deep personal loss.

On a cultural level, the war generated intense feelings of nationalism—before, during, and after the battles took place. These sentiments were often expressed through music and the arts, not only in specifically militaristic and patriotic songs but also in broader trends such as the development of national genres and forms of entertainment. Specifically, the American Songbook was fostered by the gradual emergence of what we think of as popular culture in the United States in the late nineteenth century, in forms of entertainment such as variety and minstrel shows—theatrical entertainments that involved musical performances as well as acrobatic acts and comedians. These were distinctly American phenomena, not only in form and structure but also in musical style. For example, they played a pivotal role in the career of American songwriters like Stephen Foster, who was among the first in the United States to actually enjoy professional status and success in that role. Songs like his "Beautiful Dreamer" and "My Old Kentucky Home" have retained a certain iconic status in American culture as musical expressions of our national identity.

Of course, Foster's songs are also plagued by the way in which our national identity emerged in the nineteenth century. In order to distinguish American music from its European counterparts, composers had to look to something other than the nation's European roots. To put it another way, borrowing musical styles and gestures from the music of widely represented immigrant groups like Germans, English, and French would not result in something much different than European music. As such, Foster and his contemporaries looked to the music of underrepresented groups, especially African Americans. Unfortunately, the racial prejudice of the nineteenth century meant that this appropriation was, more often than not, done in unfavorable ways. For example, Foster penned a number of songs written in Negro dialect to be performed by actors wearing blackface—an opportunity for the theatrical caricature of African Americans as unintelligent, lazy, and clownish.

By the early twentieth century, such overtly racist practices were becoming less common—though blackface would not disappear from popular culture until the middle of the century. Composers in a wide variety of arenas continued to borrow gestures from African American musical culture, however, and they rarely did so in a way that actually acknowledged the original source of inspiration. In short, the identity of mainstream popular music in the United States was increasingly being rooted in African American styles such as ragtime and jazz, even though relatively few Americans of European descent knew about the work of the black songwriters and musicians behind this development.

To be sure, African American music was not the only source material being used to forge an identity for American popular song in the early part of the twentieth century. Jewish music also proved to be especially influential—not only because many prominent songwriters (not to mention performers) of this period were of Jewish origin but also because the traditional music of their culture provided an interesting and provocative complement to that of African Americans. These two musical cultures share some common gestures, including the blending of major and minor modes within a single phrase—a trait that to the casual listener seems to capture the blend of pain and pleasure, struggle and joy that these two peoples have endured throughout their respective histories. Alternatively, most European music is written either in one mode or in the other, changing only between lengthy sections. Yet Jewish music also offered enough distinctive musical ideas, when combined as a source of inspiration with African American music and various forms of European music, to create something truly unique to American culture. In fact, bringing together different cultures in musical form represented American society in a way that no single musical tradition could have accomplished.

The unique musical mix that was coming to define American culture by the 1910s was therefore a major force in the genesis of the American Songbook specifically. It not only shaped the work of individual songwriters; it was actually cemented by most of them. Many were recent immigrants of Jewish heritage who also knew and interacted with African American musicians early in their lives. Moreover, they had both financial and artistic reasons to seek out a mainstream audience, making them especially keen to create music that would speak to a broad swath of the American public. As a result, the American Songbook became a testament not only to their own skill as songwriters but also to their place in American culture and its nationalistic mood in the early twentieth century.

Of course, not every contributor to the American Songbook fit into this category. Cole Porter grew up in a wealthy family in Indiana, far removed from the lower east side of New York City where Irving Berlin and the Gershwin brothers saw their own Jewish roots mixed into those of other immigrant groups as well as those of the African Americans living there. But Porter immersed himself in this environment later in life, enabling him to combine its musical language with his own sharp wit. Similarly, Johnny Mercer was raised on a plantation in rural Georgia, making his earliest musical influences different from those that shaped many of his older peers. Yet his southern origins exposed Mercer to African American music in a deep way, which is probably why it shaped his songwriting even more than most contributors to the American Songbook.

The American Songbook was thus born out of the desire to define American cultural identity in the early twentieth century—a desire that had begun decades earlier but was heightened considerably as the immigrant population soared and the prospect of the First World War approached. This repertoire helped foster a connection between popular music and jazz as it was created, a trend that reflects not only the continued interest among white Americans to express their identity through the appropriation of black culture but also the reality that these two cultural spheres—and their respective musical styles—were actually coming together in new ways. During the years when the American Songbook was created, Americans of different backgrounds were beginning to interact more than they had in the past. White audiences were actually encountering the work of black musicians, both on record and in person. As a result, the American Songbook was being influenced by this music in deeper ways than most popular songs written in earlier periods. Conversely, these songs became templates in the world of jazz, helping it achieve wider and broader exposure—and continuing the cycle of mutual influence.

MUSIC AND TECHNOLOGY

The early twentieth century was also a time of great technological development. Specifically, the development of sound recording played a pivotal role in establishing the kind of creative environment that would nurture the American Songbook. Thomas Edison introduced the possibility of musical recording in the 1880s with his preliminary phonograph, but the original product was not capable of making records in any kind of practical way. It took a period of both technological development and cultural acceptance for recorded music to become part of popular culture. But by the 1910s, as the earliest selections from the American Songbook were emerging, they were also being captured on record.

The increasing availability of recorded music over the next three decades had a tremendous impact on American culture. In his book *Capturing Sound: How Technology Has Changed Music*, Mark Katz has even cited seven specific ways in which recording technology changed the way we listen to and experience music: *tangibility* (we can feel, touch, and own a specific musical performance), *portability* (we can take music with us wherever we go—a trait that has only increased thanks to advancements in digital sound), *invisibility* (we can hear the musicians without actually seeing them, which has a variety of effects on our perception of both the music and the musicians), *repeatability* (we can listen to the exact same performance repeatedly), *temporality* (the original time limits of recordings ultimately created a standard length for popular songs of three to four minutes), and *manipulability* (in more recent years, recording artists have been able to do more than record a single take; they have been able to change, edit, and sample from different performances to create something not possible in live performance).

Of these, tangibility, repeatability, and temporality have probably had the deepest effects on the repertoire we call the American Songbook. The tangibility of recordings, for instance, contributed to a more widespread—and more lucrative—distribution of popular music than ever before. Although recordings have largely replaced sheet music today, it initially offered the public a second, complementary way to purchase music for their own enjoyment in their own homes. In short, it brought songwriters additional revenue for their work and enabled a wide variety of performers to gain an audience with the American public at large—not only those living close enough to theaters where they could appear in person. To put it another way, recording technology helped foster the development of a popular music for the masses, one that would be performed by many and heard by even more.

The repeatability of recordings would also change the way listeners experience and define popular songs. As recorded music became more and more common, listeners began to think of a specific recorded performance as the song itself. Instead of a template for performance consisting of melody and lyrics, the concept of a song would gradually become a single, repeatable version from a particular artist. As a result, the public gradually began to associate songs primarily with the singers who recorded them rather than the composers and lyricists who created them. This ultimately created an industry in which versions other than the one most prominently in the public ear—which was not always the first one made but rather the one that was most widely distributed—came to be conceptualized as cover versions or imitations.

On a very basic level, the temporal limits of sound recordings during the period when most of the American Songbook was written—between 1920 and 1950—also helped to shape the average length of these songs and, perhaps more importantly, how they were recorded. For example, verses were often omitted from the recorded versions of these songs in order to feature the chorus—which was in most cases the most memorable and essential part of the song. To be sure, temporal limitations were not the only reason for this practice. Verses were also written primarily as an introduction to these songs in their theatrical context, something that was obviously absent in the recording studio and in the homes of listeners. Yet even this ultimately stems from the special nature of recorded music—in this case, the invisibility of the performers.

Of course, recorded sound also led to the development of sound films, another technology that played a major role in distributing the American Songbook to the public beginning in the late 1920s. Not only did it add yet another way for the music to be marketed; it also worked in tandem with other media in the industry at this time, allowing the same songs to be experienced in every possible way—in print and in live performance, on record and on screen. In fact, the different media of the age—which also included radio broadcasts—generally operated as separate cogs in a single entertainment machine. Instead of competing with one another, they supported one another and created a much larger audience for a single song than had ever been possible before— not to mention one that could be reached much more quickly. This not only increased the potential revenue for any given song; it also vastly increased the number of listeners who would hear it. And it is this audience that served as the sounding board—in a very literal sense—for the American Songbook as it was created.

CREATING AN AMERICAN SONGBOOK

In these and other ways, the time was ripe for reaching a broad, all-encompassing American audience for popular song. To be sure, demographics were recognized in both the culture and the industry, but they were generally downplayed rather than emphasized. The widespread use of labels like "ragtime" and "jazz" for very different kinds of music between the 1910s and the 1940s demonstrates this clearly. They were applied to everything from the heavily syncopated music of African American musicians like Scott Joplin and James Reese Europe to songs that capitalized on the popularity of ragtime rather than really capturing its flavor. This includes songs like Irving Berlin's "Alexander's Ragtime Band," which describes the national fervor for ragtime and has a jaunty rhythmic character—not to mention other interesting musical qualities—but very little syncopation.

Yet "Alexander's Ragtime Band" carried enormous weight in American popular culture when Berlin published it in 1911. It had just enough ragtime sensibility to give it a distinctly American character, but its predictable, repetitive structure and tunefulness made it more widely accessible than the more frenetic ragtime compositions from African American songwriters and bandleaders. And it would be this kind of "appeal to the mainstream" approach—one that captures some of the diversity of American musical culture in a highly marketable package—that Berlin, his contemporaries, and his younger peers would follow for the next few decades.

What they gradually added to the formula, of course, were less ephemeral lyrics—ones that would not only increase the broad applicability of the songs in their own time but also extend the life of their cultural relevance. For example, "Alexander's Ragtime Band" continues to be familiar by virtue of its historical significance, but its lyrics ultimately place it in its own time. Alternatively, Irving Berlin's "Blue Skies"—which is structurally and musically similar to "Alexander's Ragtime Band"—is a popular standard that has endured not simply as an important piece of musical history but as a song that continues to resonate with contemporary listeners.

This is true for the entire repertoire we call the American Songbook, which is why singers like Michael Bublé and Tony Bennett have been largely successful in their efforts to make it music for the masses once again. Their timeless characteristics have enabled these songs to endure not just as historical artifacts but as relevant musical templates for contemporary interpreters and listeners alike. They were forged by cultural developments at a particular point in history, but they have remained a part of American popular culture because those developments created music with the ability to last.

I

ESSENTIALS OF THE AMERICAN SONGBOOK

The American Songbook is an unofficial collection of songs, most of which were written in the United States between the 1920s and the 1950s. It includes such titles as "It Had to Be You," "Over the Rainbow," "Night and Day," "Our Love Is Here to Stay," and "The Way You Look Tonight." While there is no definitive list of selections in the songbook, there is general consensus about its contents and the important musical traits these songs share.

Among the most audible of these is a tuneful, catchy melody—one that can be remembered after just one or two hearings. This trait is partially rooted in the theatrical origins of these songs. After all, the marketability of a song introduced in the theater of the early twentieth century depended largely upon a listener's ability to remember it afterward. Audiences did not have the option of buying a recorded replica of the live performance; they had to remember something of the music and lyrics in order to find and purchase it as sheet music. This requires a melody that stands out from every other part of the musical performance.

This distinguishes the American Songbook from a large portion of contemporary popular music, a genre that has come to be defined by the soundscapes made possible in the recording studio. Hip-hop, for instance, often has no melody, relying instead on the rhythmic performance of lyrics and a strong bass line beat to capture the listener's attention. To be sure, there are still songs written today with a strong melodic component, including some that even strive to emulate the American Songbook in some way. But they are as much defined by how that melody is rendered as by its actual contour of notes and rhythms. In large part, this is true simply because it is no longer necessary to write a song where the melody itself is so important. In the age of recorded music, songs can be defined in a myriad of other ways, and today's artists are taking full advantage of these options.

Of course, a truly tuneful melody is also an artful craft. Composing music of any kind requires a range of musical skills, but writing a good melody seems like a genuinely intuitive ability. Fortunately for us, the songwriters who created the American Songbook were enormously gifted in this area. The simplicity of their melodies is what made them memorable and marketable, but the quality of what they wrote is what has made them timeless. It is not easy to be simple and concise as well as striking, clever, or eloquent—as many of these songs are. In other words, the compositional prowess of these individuals is also at the heart of what makes these songs work so well and what makes them appeal to so many different listeners.

Their general intelligence also enabled them to weave their melodies into structures that emphasized their tunefulness and helped make them even easier to remember. Repetition in music is the key to shaping a listener's recognition of the tune, and these songs rely heavily on this principle. And yet, without some sort of contrast, repetition loses its value and becomes boring. The songwriters behind this repertoire therefore crafted their melodies into phrase combinations that offered frequent repetition and just enough change to make the song interesting. More often than not, this took the form of a four-phrase structure that can be represented as AABA. This simply means that the first, second, and fourth phrases (A) are melodic repetitions—either the same or very similar—and the third (B) is melodically distinct.

This structure is found throughout much of the American Songbook, and it serves to support the melody and make it even more memorable. In other words, this trait stems from the same need to market these songs in the theater through a mode of performance that is never exactly the same twice. In this context, the melody and its overall structure had to define—and sell—the song.

Another key component of this repertoire is a set of lyrics with a universally understood message. These are songs about things that everyone feels and everyone understands—things like romantic attachment, hope for the future, and even the joy of music. As such, these songs reflect the time and place in which they were written, not by speaking to its issues directly but by speaking to every kind of listener within it. This was a time when speaking to a mass audience was not only more profitable; it was also more practical. Lyricists who could capture a universal sentiment could insert their work into different theatrical shows and films—and still have a song that could also stand on its own.

Over time, of course, the broad applicability of the lyrics in these songs has made their enduring popularity possible. They are not dated in their content. Instead, they speak to feelings and ideas that are profoundly human. This makes them seem as much a part of contemporary culture as of the age in which they were written. They can sound as fresh and as new today as they did to listeners from a century past. To put it another way, these are not songs that are important simply because they were once popular. These are songs that are important because they remain both popular and relevant.

Beyond these basics, the American Songbook as a whole also exhibits a wide variety of traits common to jazz. The reason for this is quite simply that the American Songbook was emerging at the same time as jazz and the two were therefore being shaped by some of the same cultural shifts. The search for an American musical identity had long involved some sort of appropriation of African American musical ideas. The American Songbook was in many ways a continuation of this effort; jazz was instead a reaction to it, one that aimed to demonstrate African American musical ideas in their own right. Moreover, as they grew out of this circumstance simultaneously, the two musical worlds were mingling and shaping one another at every turn. Jazz articulated its identity by drawing heavily on the African American musical styles that came before it, including traditional spirituals and blues—songs filled with call-and-response gestures and a melodic and harmonic blending of major and minor modes—as well as ragtime—the energetic, highly rhythmic music popular in the first two decades of the twentieth century and noted for its wealth of syncopation. The American Songbook developed its identity by sprinkling in some of these things for a distinctly American flavor.

All of these various traits—prominent and tuneful melodies, easy-to-follow structures, widely applicable lyrics, and the general influence of jazz—can be seen throughout the American Songbook. Two textbook selections—"Blue Skies" and "I Got Rhythm"—illustrate their more conventional use, and three others—"Night and Day," "All the Things You Are," and "The Best Is Yet to Come"—exhibit them in more unusual ways. This range of approaches shows that while all these songs share a creative aesthetic, they are not entirely formulaic. They are instead a representative sample of a vibrant song collection—one that is cohesive yet varied in its musical qualities.

"BLUE SKIES"

Irving Berlin dedicated "Blue Skies" to his eldest daughter shortly after her birth in 1926, and it captures the happiness he must have felt in the early days of fatherhood. Its message is beautifully expressed through metaphors and allusions, but its meaning is simple: bad times are gone, and the good ones are here to stay. Such a sentiment could resonate with anyone, and in the hands of a natural talent like Irving Berlin, it resulted in an immensely popular song. Early renditions include those from Belle Baker in the Broadway musical comedy *Betsy*—which featured a score otherwise written by Richard Rodgers and Lorenz Hart— and Al Jolson in the landmark film musical *The Jazz Singer*. Recordings from swing bands led by Benny Goodman and Tommy Dorsey as well as singers such as Bing Crosby and Ella Fitzgerald helped to keep the song in the public ear for decades longer.

The chorus of "Blue Skies" follows that musical structure used throughout much of the American Songbook—AABA. Here, the lyrics emphasize the melodic pattern. For example, each A phrase in "Blue Skies" begins with the same two words: "blue skies." Alternatively, the B phrase begins with something different: "Never saw . . . " Melodically, the A phrases begin with a large leap upward, a gesture that emphasizes the repeated lyric and, of course, the title of the song. Alternatively, the B phrase begins with a fluid, upward-moving flourish that complements but contrasts with the A phrases.

Much has been made of Berlin's musical play on the word "blue" in the song and understandably so. In the lyrics, for instance, he uses it to describe both color and mood. He manages to invoke both the positive and negative moods associated with the color without confusing the listener. In the opening A phrase, "blue" is the color of a calm and beautiful sky while in the closing A phrase, it is the color of trouble and heartache. Thus, "blue" represents both the protagonist's painful past as well as his anticipation of a bright future. Of course, the color also suggests the music known as the blues, a style closely linked to jazz—especially jazz of the 1920s. Berlin makes the most of this meaning as well, incorporating elements of blues and jazz into his otherwise popular song such as syncopated rhythms and, perhaps more notably, the mixing of major and minor modes. This device is used in the blues to denote the expression of both pleasure and pain. This is because the major mode is widely used to evoke and express positive emotions and the minor mode is more often used for negative ones. Here, Berlin does much the same thing, though he alternates between the two—in accordance with his lyrics—rather than bending the all-important third pitch as is common in blues.

Of course, some performers of "Blue Skies" have played with the third pitch a bit more freely. Others have interpreted the song's melody and rhythms in different ways, adding and omitting material as they see fit. And yet, the original tune somehow remains despite these adjustments. This shows the influence of jazz on the song in another way—its usefulness as a basis for improvisation. To some extent, this malleability also stems from the need for versatility within the music industry. After all, a song premiered on stage would in all likelihood need to be arranged for sheet music quite differently than it would for a screen adaptation or a recording session. The fact that so many performers of the period felt free to interpret songs like "Blue Skies" with such liberty, however, is ultimately attributable to the way in which jazz was reshaping popular music as a whole. The fact that "Blue Skies"—and other American Songbook selections—caught the attention of so many jazz artists shows how a songwriting industry once catering to the stage was now meeting the needs of a much wider musical marketplace.

Oddly enough, musical simplicity is what made all of this possible. Simple musical statements are, after all, the ones best suited to both improvisational treatment and rearrangement. And the American Songbook is filled with the best kind of simplicity—the kind that is evident in "Blue Skies." It is a rich and poignant song that does not need embellishment, but it can also easily withstand it. This, along with its timeless message of optimism, has made it one of the most beloved songs of the twentieth century.

"I GOT RHYTHM"

George and Ira Gershwin's "I Got Rhythm" is another classic example from the American Songbook. Its lyrics also convey a timeless message, one that celebrates the good things in life—most notably love and music. It has been used in a variety of dramatic circumstances as well as enjoyed on its own. Among its most memorable renditions are those from Ethel Merman in the song's Broadway premiere, *Girl Crazy* (1930); Judy Garland in the film adaptation of *Girl Crazy* (1943); Gene Kelly in the classic film *An American in Paris* (1952); and Ella Fitzgerald in her album *Ella Fitzgerald Sings the George and Ira Gershwin Songbook* (1959). Many more versions have been performed and recorded over the years, of course, but even these four demonstrate the song's versatility and longevity. On stage, on screen, and on its own, "I Got Rhythm" has been heard by generations of listeners.

The song's lyrics provide the proper backdrop for such universal enjoyment, and they follow the same AABA pattern used in "Blue Skies." Just like in the Berlin song, each A phrase begins with the same words—"I got"—and then proceeds with a list of possessions the protagonist relishes—rhythm, music, flowers, stars, dreams, and, of course, love. The B phrase, however, breaks with this pattern. Here, the lyrics refer to what the protagonist does not have—troubles. Not surprisingly, George Gershwin follows the pattern of his brother's lyrics by using a melodic line for each A phrase that moves note by note up and down the scale—with a brief flourish at the conclusion. For the contrasting B phrase, Gershwin uses a different melodic contour, one that, instead of moving up and down, remains very still. Thus, the music reinforces the pattern set forth by the lyrics.

The simplicity of the song's message and its melody are complemented by vigorous rhythmic activity—one of the song's jazz elements. For example, each of the ascending and descending lines is set to a syncopated rhythmic pattern; in fact, only one of the articulations in each of these phrases falls on the beat. And—despite its distinct melodic structure—the B segment employs these same rhythms. This rhythmic gesture thus ties the two contrasting segments together and, not insignificantly, makes the song's title especially poignant.

It also communicates the joy associated with rhythmic liberty at the time the song was written. This aspect of jazz was a big part of what intrigued white American listeners in the 1920s, and not just because it was fresh to the ear. It offered something new for the body as well. The rhythmic vitality of jazz had ushered in dances like the Charleston and the Black Bottom in which dancers incorporated their bodies rather than just their feet. In short, the freer approach to rhythm in the music of jazz came to represent physical freedom as well. It is little wonder, then, that the Gershwins chose to make rhythm and happiness—including romantic happiness and the physical joy that accompanies it—synonymous. The association was already entrenched in popular music culture at the time; they just created a song about it.

"NIGHT AND DAY"

Cole Porter wrote the music and lyrics for "Night and Day" shortly after the Gershwins penned "I Got Rhythm." Fred Astaire was the first to introduce Porter's number to the public, and he did so in a single dramatic vehicle—on stage in 1932 (*Gay Divorce*) and on screen in 1934 (*The Gay Divorcee*). It then became one of the first songs recorded by Frank Sinatra as well as a featured selection for such notables as Bing Crosby and Doris Day. It remains one of Porter's best-known and most beloved songs.

The song's lyrics are what anyone would expect from a standard. They speak to the overwhelming and enduring power of love. As the title suggests, the protagonist is consumed with thoughts of love at every hour. Porter's words also set the structure of his song, which in this case is one with fluid boundaries between phrases. His use of the same words—those of the song's title—at the beginning and end of each phrase makes this possible, though his musical craftsmanship is ultimately what makes it work. For one thing, his melodic phrases are closely related. The distinct pitches he uses in each are unique, of course, but—unlike those in "I Got Rhythm"—they all move in a similar, sinuous fashion. Porter also departs from the typical AABA pattern in favor of ABABCB. This lengthier, interwoven structure allows the listener to drift through a blend of repetition and contrast rather than encounter a single burst of difference. Porter's rhythmic choices contribute even more continuous movement to the song. For example, he includes a number of triplet figures, where three tones are articulated in the usual space of two. This creates a sense of freedom or looseness in the timing, something that interpreters have often emphasized.

Of course, Porter had good reason to use all of these techniques: they poignantly communicate his lyrics. As a result of his compositional prowess, the song's sense of continual longing is heard not only in the words but also in the music. Its muted boundaries are the musical demonstration of the protagonist's thoughts and feelings. There are pauses and changes of direction, but nothing that actually represents a break.

The influence of jazz is not especially strong in "Night and Day," though it is certainly evident in some of its most familiar interpretations. For example, Frank Sinatra's well-known version with the Nelson Riddle Orchestra (1956) has numerous characteristics listeners would expect from a big band jazz record. It also has been rendered by prominent jazz artists such as Art Tatum and Oscar Peterson. The reason for this is both the song's relative simplicity and the connection between jazz and the popular standard that has been nurtured and developed over time.

"ALL THE THINGS YOU ARE"

Jerome Kern and Oscar Hammerstein II had collaborated on and off for more than a decade when they wrote "All the Things You Are" for the 1939 stage musical *Very Warm for May*. Though the show did not please critics or the general public, the song has long been acclaimed by both. Early recordings by the big bands of Tommy Dorsey and Artie Shaw helped it gain an initial hearing when the show failed. Singers including Frank Sinatra and Ella Fitzgerald then made it familiar to even more listeners, and jazz artists as diverse as Dizzy Gillespie, Django Reinhardt, Gerry Mulligan, and Dave Brubeck—not to mention many others—have made the song a standard backdrop for improvisation in the jazz repertoire.

"All the Things You Are" is often noted for its unusually rich harmonic movement. Indeed, this complex facet of the song is likely one of the reasons it has proven especially popular with jazz musicians; more frequent chord changes—as well as chords consisting of more pitches, such as seventh and ninth chords—give improvisers more notes from which to choose. Kern also wrote a beautiful and interesting melody, however—one that helps to propel the harmonic movement underneath.

This melody adheres to the basic AABA structure but with significant variation in each of the A phrases. Rather than repeat his opening phrase, Kern sets a basic melodic architecture in the first statement upon which he can build three similar yet distinct musical lines. The first and second A phrases, for instance, differ in their starting pitches and their concluding figures. After the contrasting B phrase, the final A phrase recalls the opening but then finishes the song with something entirely new.

The overall sense of Kern's melody is one of spaciousness. The large leaps and extended range contribute to this feeling, as do the shifts in motion. Combined with such sprawling harmonic movement, the song is expansive in its communicative power. Perhaps Kern was simply experimenting with the limits of the popular song form—retaining its familiar structure but going beyond its typical melodic and harmonic language. Or perhaps he was inspired by his collaborator's lyrics to write something that would express their emotional breadth and depth in musical terms. After all, they are more serious and sophisticated than most lyrics in the American Songbook, making them especially well-suited to more complex music. Regardless, the result is an exceptional song that nevertheless embodies all the qualities of a popular standard. Its subject is both universal and optimistic, its structure is easily audible, and its musical language incorporates elements of jazz—in this case, harmonies rather than rhythms.

"THE BEST IS YET TO COME"

Cy Coleman and Carolyn Leigh wrote "The Best Is Yet to Come" in 1959, making it one of the latest examples from the American Songbook. As such, it is both a continuation of earlier songwriting practices as well as a demonstration of how those practices were changing by the middle of the century. One noteworthy distinction, for instance, is that "The Best Is Yet to Come" was not composed for a musical. Instead, it was originally popularized by recordings, including ones from Tony Bennett, Peggy Lee, and Frank Sinatra. It nevertheless exudes the style of songs from earlier Broadway and Hollywood musicals, which is why these kinds of voices were the ones to render them—and why singers like Broadway star Brian Stokes Mitchell and neo-crooner Michael Bublé have been the ones to record them in more recent years.

Carolyn Leigh's lyrics for "The Best Is Yet to Come" are much like those of earlier standards. They are highly optimistic in spirit, anticipating the joy of a romance yet to be experienced. Notably, this message not only demonstrates the enduring influence of earlier songwriting trends, it also makes the song universally applicable—even if the music industry did not need it to be so by the late 1950s.

Structurally, "The Best Is Yet to Come" follows a modified version of the conventional AABA pattern. As in "All the Things You Are," the same basic pattern is there, but each A phrase is treated differently. Even more innovative is Coleman's unusually complex melodic line. The opening segment of the A phrase, for instance, teeters back and forth between a stationary low note and a sequence of chromatically descending pitches above it. This creates a disjointed feeling and makes it difficult for a listener to remember on first hearing. Because Coleman repeats this material twice in each of the opening A sections, however, the line becomes recognizable. Even though the melodic material is more experimental, its frequent recurrence yields much the same memorable effect on the listener as a song with a more conventional melody.

Jazz elements also abound in "The Best Is Yet to Come," giving it even stronger ties to the American Songbook and making it especially useful to jazz musicians borrowing from it. Coleman himself was one of these, so it is hardly surprising that he wrote highly syncopated rhythms used to articulate his melody. His long successions of off-the-beat attacks make the song feel even more disjointed and bumpy—though only temporarily. He concludes each segment with a long note that provides a pause in the melodic and rhythmic movement. This ending note is preceded by a melodic slide downward in pitch—another jazz technique that brings both smoothness and closure.

Despite its later date of composition, "The Best Is Yet to Come" exemplifies the traits of the American Songbook and the cultural phenomena that shaped it as much as any other song in the collection. Its melodic and harmonic material is a bit more adventurous than some earlier selections, but it is nevertheless tuneful thanks to its familiar pattern of repetition and contrast. It also incorporates a number of jazz elements, a practice that by 1959—in the age of rock and roll—associated it even more with earlier songwriting. Most importantly, though, it exudes the optimistic, romantic spirit of earlier twentieth-century music.

DIFFERENCES AND SIMILARITIES

These five songs were written over the course of four decades by songwriters with different personalities, strengths, and approaches to making music. Even so, they all demonstrate how the expanding music industry of the early twentieth century, the optimism of the age, and the rise of jazz infused the American Songbook. The musical traits they share, from structural similarities to likenesses in their lyrics, all stem from these cultural influences.

Notably, these songs also show us how these influences worked together rather than separately. Consider, for instance, their melodic simplicity. This trait not only lends itself to the kind of catchiness desired by the music business; it also facilitates creativity on the part of the performer, which in turn leads to different renditions—each of which can be marketed on its own value. Similarly, the inclusion of syncopated rhythms not only made these songs attractive to listeners interested in jazz music; it also made them especially useful in dramatic contexts involving dance. In short, these influences were not operating independently but collectively to shape the music of their time.

One other trait that most standards share is a verse that is so distinct from the song's chorus that it is often omitted, both in performance and, perhaps more notably, in the collective memory of the song. The verse of "Blue Skies," for instance, is rarely heard and therefore largely forgotten. One reason for this is simply that the verse was written primarily to serve the original theatrical context. It provided a transition into the song, providing a bit of narrative and a musical introduction. As

"Blue Skies" moved out of the theater and into the American conscious-ness, the verse was dropped and the more tuneful chorus was pre-served. The verse of "I Got Rhythm," on the other hand, is a little more familiar, in large part because it has been heard on stage and screen more frequently than the Berlin number. Its chorus is still more widely recognized than its verse, but the two have remained linked as a result of its dramatic usage.

Of course, the main reason that these songs are defined by their choruses is that they provide the catchiest music and most memorable sentiments. And this is where they met the needs of the music industry. Their verses show far more individuality, which from an artistic stand-point is significant, of course. But, as a cultural phenomenon, it is their choruses that illustrate how music was being made, marketed, and con-sumed in the early twentieth century.

2

AUTHORS OF THE AMERICAN SONGBOOK

The men and women who wrote the American Songbook were masters of essential songwriting techniques. Its composers understood how to construct a melody, set it harmonically and rhythmically, and make it fit with a lyric. Its lyricists understood how to communicate familiar messages in clever ways—as well as in meaningful and beautiful words. Notably, though, they were also very much a part of the time in which they lived—a time characterized by a rapidly changing entertainment industry, a generally optimistic spirit (whether as a celebration of joy or an escape from hardship), and a good deal of stylistic musical exchange. They were not working outside of or against this environment but rather from within it—and they allowed their work to be shaped by it as a result.

The combination of these traits has resulted in a musical collection of both quality and cultural significance. If its authors had not been exceptional musicians, their work might have garnered some initial listeners but would probably have faded from memory. Likewise, if these songwriters had not responded to the world around them, they might have gained some posterity in the long run but would likely not have enjoyed much success in their own lifetimes. Instead, their work was both musically interesting and widely popular in its own time.

To put it another way, these writers used their talents in ways that corresponded to the demands of the music industry and the American public at the time. They were not pandering in any way; they were

simply responding creatively to the situation in which they found themselves. For example, many of them became especially adept at configur-
ing a song into a dramatic situation without making it required. Similarly, they could craft a song with a particular singer in mind that could
nevertheless be rendered just as memorably by others—including instrumentalists. Some even managed to include timely references and
themes in their songs without making them seem dated. All of these
techniques and more demonstrate how creativity and practicality need
not be in conflict with one another. They can, in fact, drive one another.

Moreover, these men and women were gifted at expressing something beyond the literal meaning of a song's lyrics—something that
could reach the heart as well as the head, future generations as well as
the present one. The songs discussed in the previous chapter have
already revealed how the music of these songs often works beautifully
as a vehicle for lyrics, and the successful combination of the two can be
seen in both collaborations and in songs whose music and words were
created by the same person. Even more impressive, though, is how this
music can also speak on its own—in part because the lyrics to which it is
so well-suited have helped it gain familiarity, but also because the music
itself has something to say. This is why the repertoire has proven so
useful and interesting to instrumentalists as well as singers—which in
turn has led to a range of both performers and listeners that few other
musical collections can claim.

What follows is a discussion of some noteworthy examples of musical
craftsmanship in the American Songbook, organized according to topic.
To be sure, there are more songs that could fit into each category and
songwriters whose talents go beyond the one in which they are discussed. But this is an attempt to provide an overview of what makes the
American Songbook more than just a collection of songs with similar
traits shaped by the same cultural forces. It is also a collection of exceptionally well-written songs produced by gifted composers and lyricists in
response to these forces.

WRITING FOR ANY CONTEXT

Writing a song within a story is not an easy task. For one thing, the
dramatic situation has to be conducive to the inclusion of a song. Unless

the entire story is sung, as in opera, there must be some sort of reason for the characters to sing—or at the very least be listening to music. Backstage musicals, those in which the characters are musical performers in a show within the show, make this relatively easy—and the abundance of this type of musical on both stage and screen attests to its practicality in this regard. Yet many selections from the American Songbook were written for other types of contexts, ones that required a little more craftsmanship to make them work. For example, the songwriters need to find lyrics and a musical style suited not only to the actor or actress but to the character. After all, if the language of the song is either too lofty or too simple for the character singing it, it loses both sincerity and credibility. They also need to write for the precise moment in the story that will introduce the song. They have to capture the emotional state of the character in that circumstance and, in many cases, help him or her transition into the next one.

Given this level of specificity, it is especially impressive that so many selections in the American Songbook have not only been successful additions to the dramatic situations for which they were written but have also proven tremendously popular outside of these contexts. Among the strongest examples of this is "Over the Rainbow," written by Harold Arlen and E. Y. Harburg for the landmark film *The Wizard of Oz*. Harburg's lyrics are perfectly suited to the youthful and wide-eyed Dorothy in both spirit and content. They capture her innocence, her imagination, and her desire to move beyond her present circumstances. As she looks out at the plain landscape before her feeling rather glum, she sings about the magical and colorful world of her dreams. It seems entirely plausible for a young girl to do this, both as a way to cheer herself temporarily and in the genuine hope that she might be able to visit this world—which, of course, she does.

Harold Arlen's musical setting of "Over the Rainbow" takes this dreaminess a step further, painting a picture of this world even before viewers of the film are taken there. The opening ascending leap in his melody, for instance, is a musical gesture that captures the idea of going up and over. Then, his circular continuation of the line maintains a sense of buoyancy—as opposed to dropping or falling. All of this creates a musical sensibility that matches Dorothy's imaginative mood and her desire to soar beyond reality.

At the same time, Arlen does not complicate the melody to the point that it seems too sophisticated for a young girl to sing. To complement the large movements in his opening A segment, he writes a B segment that moves very simply—back and forth between alternating pitches that are closely spaced. This reminds the listener of who is singing—a girl who has grand and vivid dreams but who is limited in her actual life experiences.

For all of these reasons, "Over the Rainbow" is ideally suited to its original context. Yet it has also proven enormously appealing beyond this context. Two things make this possible. First, Harburg's lyrics rely on general imagery to convey Dorothy's dreams. By referring to things like clear skies and bluebirds, he makes the song applicable for almost any kind of wishful thinking. Second, Arlen provides the listener with musical conventions that make the song stylistically and structurally familiar rather than something uniquely for Dorothy. These include the AABA pattern of repetition and contrast as well as the kind of melodic and harmonic movement listeners would expect. In short, the traits of "Over the Rainbow" that make it part of the American Songbook are also what make it work so well outside of its original context.

To put it another way, consider how "Over the Rainbow" compares to the other songs Harburg and Arlen wrote for *The Wizard of Oz*—songs like "Follow the Yellow Brick Road" or "Ding-Dong! The Witch Is Dead." While equally familiar to fans of the film, these other songs from Harburg and Arlen have not enjoyed the same kind of life outside their original context as "Over the Rainbow," and the reason is that they do not fit the profile of the standard popular song. Most obviously, their lyrics refer to specific characters and happenings in the story. As such, they lack the kind of universal expression in "Over the Rainbow." In addition, their musical structures are designed around their respective places in the film rather than relying on an AABA framework. This makes them very well-suited to the story but not as easily extracted from it.

What Harburg and Arlen accomplished with "Over the Rainbow" is therefore noteworthy. They created a song for a specific dramatic situation that nevertheless had much broader applicability. Of course, they are not unique in this achievement. Other songwriters of the time succeeded in doing this as well, including George and Ira Gershwin. In fact, the Gershwins were so adept at writing both for and beyond a story that many of their songs have not only been extracted from their original dramatic contexts; they have also been reworked into new ones. The 1951 film *An American in Paris* and the 1992 Broadway musical *Crazy for You* are among the best-known examples of this phenomenon. Notably, "I Got Rhythm" appears in both of these contexts, and it fits remarkably well in each one. In the former, it is performed by the film's leading character—an American artist named Jerry Mulligan—as part of a playful conversation with a group of Parisian children curious about American culture. This makes the song's appearance almost like a cameo; Mulligan uses it not as an expression of his own exuberance but as a symbol of American life—as well as an opportunity to showcase other American things like tap dancing. In the latter, "I Got Rhythm" is used in a more conventional manner; it is the closing song and dance number of the first act. It celebrates the brighter future the characters—especially Polly Baker, the female lead—now have, even though unforeseen complications lie ahead. Its optimistic spirit is thus an ideal match for the situation.

These are examples of musical recycling at its best, made possible by the unique qualities of the original material. After all, in order for works like *An American in Paris* and *Crazy for You* to exist, their creators had to see the extraordinary dramatic potential in the songs the Gershwin brothers had written. These were songs made to tell stories—not just one story, but many stories. This is because they convey powerful emotions in genuine ways. They can speak for different characters and to different audiences because they focus on what is shared between them—their human nature.

WRITING FOR ANY PERFORMER

The American Songbook is filled with songs suited for performance by multiple types of voices and instruments. This trait was necessary in an industry that relied on different media to popularize songs. In fact, songs were usually introduced by more than one performer or group. One singer might introduce a song on stage, another on film, and another on record. One or more instrumental versions of the latest selections were often released around the same time as vocal ones. As such, even songs that were originally intended for a particular singer—such as the star of a new show or film—had to be written in such a way that they would work well when rendered by someone else.

One of the best examples of this is "It Had to Be You" by Isham Jones and Gus Kahn. Shortly after it was written in 1924, a number of different recordings were released by various record labels—each in a different style. Marion Harris, for instance, offered listeners a bluesy interpretation that emphasized the sense of devotion and longing in the song. Alternatively, Billy Murray and Aileen Stanley performed it in a more playful manner, highlighting the song's lighthearted spirit. And quick-paced instrumental renditions from bandleaders like Paul Whiteman—as well as Isham Jones himself—underlined the rhythmic side of the song and its suitability for dancing.

In order to be this versatile, a song needs to have certain traits, one of which is a limited melodic range. This makes it easier for a wide variety of voice types and instruments to perform it. In "It Had to Be You," the melody extends just beyond an octave. Another feature that makes a song adaptable is its use of a short, recurring melodic fragment—the one to which the title lyric is set. This musical gesture appears throughout much of the song; Jones sets it at different pitch levels to provide movement and contrast, but its familiarity ties the song together and ultimately defines it. It is the song's signature, even though it is only five notes long. Such a brief motive may seem overly simple, but it actually facilities variation. (Consider, for example, Beethoven's Symphony no. 5, a richly complex piece of music based on a four-note melodic gesture.) As a bandleader and orchestrator, Jones would have understood the value of this trait, and he made it work especially well in "It Had to Be You."

Other elements of the song offer additional opportunities for interpretation. Tempo and rhythms, for instance, can easily be adjusted by the performer. Jones's melody works well at almost any moderate pace, and it can handle a little or a lot of syncopation. Notably, thanks to Gus Kahn's lyrics, this not only offers the opportunity for musical variation but also for changes in meaning. Taken at a slower tempo, his words seem more serious—as is true in Marion Harris's interpretation. With more rhythmic velocity, they feel more playful and fun—as in the recording by Billy Murray and Aileen Stanley. The message is always genuine, but Kahn crafted it so that it could apply to different kinds of romantic personalities and relationships.

"It Had to Be You" is therefore an excellent example of just how transferrable a song can be. Clearly, Isham Jones understood both the practical and artistic qualities a song would need in order to be interpreted by a wide variety of performers. And Gus Kahn knew how to write lyrics that not only conveyed a universal message but also could be infused with different kinds of sentimentality. Most authors of the American Songbook accomplished these goals to some extent, in part because it was necessary to do so. Even so, some songwriters, like Jones and Kahn, excelled at this particular endeavor. They are the reason "It Had to Be You" has enjoyed one of the longest and most varied lists of interpreters over the past century.

MAKING THE TIMELY TIMELESS

Songs with cultural references are not the norm in the American Songbook and for good reason. In order to maximize the audience for a particular song, the entertainment industry had moved away from songs on timely topics in favor of more universal ones. Still, there is at least one songwriter who alluded to the world around him in ways that we nevertheless understand today—Cole Porter.

Porter is often recognized for his wit, and it is undoubtedly a unique combination of musical, poetic, and intellectual gifts that enabled him to write as he did. This includes his ability to incorporate cultural references without limiting his audience. A quintessential example of this is Porter's "You're the Top," a song in which the protagonist compares his friend to a list of familiar beloved icons of popular culture. This could easily have dated the song if Porter had chosen only timely references. Instead, he incorporates a number of icons known not only in 1930s America but by people of different generations—and throughout the world. For example, he alludes to widely read writers such as Shakespeare and Dante, celebrated museums such as the Louvre and the National Gallery, and international landmarks such as the Tower of Pisa and the Coliseum.

He also includes contemporary references, of course, but he relies primarily on ones that were already enjoying widespread familiarity and were therefore more likely to remain household names for some time— especially since film and sound recordings were changing fame from a localized and often temporary phenomenon into a broader, more enduring one. As such, it is particularly noteworthy that Porter includes a number of figures from within the entertainment industry such as Greta Garbo, Jimmy Durante, and Fred Astaire. Whether Porter was consciously thinking about the long-term effects of new media on the life of his song is impossible to say, but he was at the very least writing with an awareness of the way they would have familiarized his initial audience with his references. And he ultimately capitalized on their role in making many American entertainers popular for generations.

Porter wrote "You're the Top" for the stage musical *Anything Goes*, which has enjoyed its own longevity through revivals and regional performances. While these subsequent versions are at least partly responsible for the enduring familiarity of the show's songs, Porter's material had to be worth revisiting in the first place. One reason for this is the general quality of his work, but another, more specific one is his ability to speak about modernity in ways that have remained relevant over time. This is especially evident in the show's title song—"Anything Goes." Here, Porter describes the broad acceptance of things once thought taboo in American society. This theme is still very much a part of popular culture today, and Porter navigates it in such a way that it can easily sound as fresh as it did to 1930s listeners. His lyrics are neither too specific nor too vague; they describe things like rising hemlines, the use of profanity, and changing gender roles in romantic relationships, all of which add distinctive details to the song without making it sound dated.

Longevity may not have been among Porter's goals when writing "You're the Top" or "Anything Goes," yet he achieved it all the same. At a time when universal expression and broad applicability were called for throughout the entertainment industry, he managed to craft a number of songs with remarkably precise meanings that nevertheless still ring true today. His astute understanding of popular culture and his own musical and lyrical talents made this possible.

MAKING AN OCCASION SONG AN ALL-OCCASION SONG

Songs for special occasions are no more common in the American Songbook than those with timely references. And yet, they are present—and they are one of its most intriguing elements. They were written for unusually specific circumstances, including not only a singer and performance context but also a particular occasion of celebration. Such limits would seem to exclude them from the American Songbook altogether. Instead, though, they have become some of its most widely known and beloved selections. This is undoubtedly because they were written by no less a talent than Irving Berlin.

"Easter Parade" and "White Christmas" are these remarkable songs, and their histories reveal just how much they are part of American popular culture. "Easter Parade," for instance, was written for and premiered in the 1933 Broadway revue *As Thousands Cheer*. It then appeared in two films featuring Berlin songs—*Alexander's Ragtime Band* (1938) and *Holiday Inn* (1942)—before becoming the centerpiece and namesake of the Fred Astaire and Judy Garland film *Easter Parade* in 1948. "White Christmas" was also introduced in *Holiday Inn* in 1942, a film that, as its name suggests, included several holiday songs. It then became the signature song of the classic film *White Christmas* in 1954. Bing Crosby, who performed the song in both films and recorded its best-selling rendition, has become synonymous with the song.

To be sure, the popularity of the films in which these songs were used—especially the most recent ones—has contributed significantly to their enduring presence in American popular culture. Even so, other songs from these films have significantly less contemporary currency, suggesting that "Easter Parade" and "White Christmas" have at least a few inherent qualities that have contributed to their special popularity. After all, on a practical level, it would have been more likely for Berlin's "Be Careful, It's My Heart"—which appeared as the Valentine's Day selection in *Holiday Inn*—to be especially popular. On the timeless theme of love, it even fits the model of an American Songbook selection more closely. After all, its playful yet profound message about the devastating impact of a broken heart could have had wide applicability. Instead, though, it is "Easter Parade" and "White Christmas" that have been the most widely enjoyed.

In both cases, the main reason for this seems to be the nostalgia Berlin captured in his music and lyrics. "Easter Parade" is, after all, a musical celebration of a simple but visible holiday tradition: dressing up in nice clothes. As Jeffrey Magee explains in his book, *Irving Berlin's American Musical Theater*, this tradition had a special place in New

York culture, a fact that contributed to how the song was originally staged in *As Thousands Cheer*. Since the late nineteenth century, the parade of well-dressed socialites on Fifth Avenue that Berlin describes in the song had been a noteworthy part of the cultural landscape—receiving the kind of media coverage now given to parades of celebrities attending awards ceremonies, in which fashion is given as much if not more attention than anything else. And yet, the specificity of Berlin's lyrics does not make them meaningless for American listeners removed from this particular tradition—whether by geography or by time. Wearing special clothes has long been part of the Easter holiday for almost everyone, and it remains a common practice today—even for those who rarely, if ever, dress up for other occasions.

By speaking to this tradition, Berlin crafted a consciously nostalgic song—that is, one designed to make listeners reminisce about the past. He even wanted to make the song sound old-fashioned, which led him to borrow melodic material from a song he wrote years before entitled "Smile and Show Your Dimple." As Benjamin Sears notes in his edited collection of essays on the songwriter, Berlin only excerpted a few segments from the song. Still, it was enough to help him achieve the desired effect—a song that looked longingly backward in both its lyrics and its music.

"White Christmas" is also inherently nostalgic. To be sure, many contemporary listeners experience it as such in part because of the role the song—and perhaps especially Bing Crosby's legendary recording of it—has played in our own holiday traditions. But, like "Easter Parade," it was also a celebration of the past even when it was first written. The song's protagonist yearns not simply for snow but for what snow at Christmastime represents—a traditional holiday. And, of course, this wish is made by someone who feels far removed from tradition. This is one reason the song was so beloved at the time Berlin wrote it. After a decade of economic depression and the start of another war, Americans were longing for anything that represented normalcy. As such, they could easily identify with the song's protagonist, remembering a time when not only Christmas but other times of the year were marked by peace and hope.

Noting the song's sorrowful sensibility, Jody Rosen evocatively characterizes it as "a lament for lost happiness"—something that is evident in both the lyrics and in the music that accompanies them. Most obviously, Berlin's protagonist makes it clear in the opening lines of the chorus that he is looking backward, reminiscing about and wishing for the kind of Christmas he has experienced in the past. To make this more convincing, Berlin keeps his imagery limited in its details. This makes the song feel even more like a memory, like snapshots of Christmases past. Berlin's melody contributes even more to this sensibility. The song's celebrated opening line meanders chromatically as if it is not quite sure where to go. This makes it sound much like the protagonist feels—a bit lost. The arching phrase that follows begins to transport him into his imagination, and the more familiar melodic contours and consonant harmonies seem to represent warmth and comfort. They are what listeners expect from a popular song, just like the protagonist's memories are what he expects from Christmas. The song moves back and forth between these two musical ideas, keeping the listener mindful of both the present and the past.

Irving Berlin was a master of many things as a songwriter, but he seems to have had a special talent for writing special occasion songs. Other composers have produced love songs as beautiful and enduringly popular as his, but none has captured the shared experiences of the American public with such clarity. His lyrics include just the right kind of details—the kind that generate meaning for a wide range of listeners—and his music communicates their timeless messages simply and transparently. Berlin has thus given the special occasion song a place in the American Songbook.

MAKING THE MUSIC SPEAK

Most standards from the American Songbook have been recorded by instrumentalists as well as by singers, and even versions featuring a singer often contain significant instrumental sections. This attests to the strength of their melodies and, more specifically, to the ability of these melodies to convey a message even when words are absent. One stellar example of this is the song "Stardust." It was written and recorded as an instrumental selection by Hoagy Carmichael in 1927. Then, in 1929, it was published with lyrics by Mitchell Parish. By the early 1930s, it was available in numerous versions—both instrumental and vocal—recorded by many of the most celebrated artists of the time.

Because it was written as instrumental music first, "Stardust" obviously works without lyrics. Still, Carmichael provided listeners—and his future collaborator—with a strikingly emotional melody. To put it another way, he gave the song its sense of longing even before Parish expressed it in words. His spiraling melody plunges downward and then reaches back up above its staring point, spanning more than an octave and taking large leaps along the way. This dramatic movement is anything but complacent. Instead, it captures both the melancholy and the hopefulness of someone who yearns for something—or in this case, someone. As such, Parish's lyrics add clarity and beauty to a song already filled with emotional depth.

Carmichael was clearly gifted at this kind of writing because he did much the same thing when he crafted "Skylark" a little more than a decade later. This time, Johnny Mercer was the one to provide lyrics for Carmichael's music. To go along with Carmichael's despondent-sounding melodic circles, Mercer crafted a character who, in desperation, asks a passing skylark for romantic advice. The combination is just as compelling as the one in "Stardust." This is only because Mercer captured the emotional quality of Carmichael's music, however. The sense of despair was already there.

In his biography of Hoagy Carmichael, Richard M. Sudhalter describes "Stardust" as a "form of musical portraiture" with "strong elicitations of time, scene, even character." This evocative characterization draws attention to what Carmichael accomplished as a musical communicator. He was, as Sudhalter suggests, much like a visual artist, able to capture and convey something remarkably real without using words. Instead, he spoke his message through notes and rhythms. Other contributors to the American Songbook were able to do this as well, though Carmichael is especially noteworthy for the strength and clarity of his musical expressions.

PUTTING IT ALL TOGETHER

The tunesmiths behind the American Songbook had a wealth of talents, only some of which have been highlighted here. Interestingly, these gifts lent themselves especially well to the production of universally enjoyable music: songs suited to different dramatic contexts and performing forces, themed songs made timeless, and melodies that communicate powerfully with or without words. To conclude this chapter, it thus makes sense to consider one more example—one that exhibits all of these traits, even to the point of self-parody.

"Isn't It Romantic" was written by Richard Rodgers and Lorenz Hart for the 1932 film *Love Me Tonight*. It is first sung by the leading male character, a custom tailor played by Maurice Chevalier. He begins by comparing the practice of sewing to a romantic relationship—the meeting of needle and thread, stitches and fabric, and so forth. He then alludes to a desire for female companionship, but his words are not traditionally romantic. Instead of beautiful imagery or emotional language, he sings about how his love will take care of him and the everyday life they will share. This is meant to be ironic, of course, because it is not what most people think of as romantic—especially in the context of a Hollywood film. It is also ultimately truthful, however. After all, the simple things one person does for another—things like making a cup of coffee or taking care of some household task—can often hold as much romantic value as more grandiose expressions of love, especially for those in long-term relationships.

The tailor's customer does not seem especially interested in the words of the song, but he does like the tune, and he continues to hum it as he leaves. A cab driver waiting outside the shop then hears it and starts singing it, substituting his own thoughts—which are entirely ordinary and not in the least romantic, ironic or otherwise. Soon, the driver has a fare who happens to be a songwriter. He also likes the melody and transcribes it into musical notation as he rides, singing only the names of the pitches rather than any words—except, of course, the title phrase. He keeps working on the song as he moves onto a train carrying soldiers, who then pick up the tune and turn it into a military march. When the soldiers move through a nearby field, their singing is overheard by a Gypsy violinist. He then plays it for his family and friends, a performance heard by a princess in her nearby castle. Finally, she sings it on her balcony, adding new lyrics that describe the kind of man she hopes will fall in love with her. Thus, it ultimately becomes the kind of romantic ballad filmgoers of the 1930s would have expected.

This staging of the song parodies the very nature of musical tunefulness and the way in which new songs move through popular culture. As a result, it is also an exaggerated expression of musical versatility. The song appears in numerous contexts that, however silly, are nevertheless feasible. It is also performed by different voices and instruments, all of which are capable of rendering the tune easily. Rodgers and Hart accomplish universality by using alternate lyrics in places and omitting them in others, but they still rely on the broad applicability of the song's title phrase and its range of meanings. And, of course, the melody conveys a message all on its own. Even without any lyrics, its opening phrase conveys a sense of closeness by beginning and ending on the same pitch and moving ever so slightly above and below it in between.

These varied dimensions of the song help us understand what makes the American Songbook special. Yes, they are well-crafted in musical terms, but they also exhibit traits unique to this repertoire—traits that helped them achieve a kind of omnipresence in American popular culture. It is not simply that they were popular; they were literally everywhere. And the characteristics that made them so transferable initially have also helped them endure. This is what makes these songs so interesting and important. Other popular songs can easily be noted for their sales figures, cultural significance, influence, and even listenership, but the standards of the American Songbook have never been equaled in their adaptability. Of course, the men and women behind the American Songbook are entirely responsible for this versatility. Without their creativity, there would be no American Songbook—only a series of song hits now faded from memory and rarely, if ever, heard.

3

THE AMERICAN SONGBOOK ON STAGE

Stage productions have long been used as a launching pad for popular songs in the United States. Operas and operettas imported from Europe were among the nineteenth-century theatrical entertainments to do this, turning excerpts from the works of Giacomo Puccini, Arthur Sullivan, and many more into popular hits. Minstrel and variety shows did much the same for American songwriters like Stephen Foster and his contemporaries. Then, by the turn of the twentieth century, vaudeville and revues had joined the list of theatrical genres introducing songs to American listeners.

The music publishing industry helped, of course, providing audiences with the means to reproduce selections from these varied productions in their own homes. But it was often the shows themselves that were the driving force. Sheet music helped keep the songs popular, but the theater was the way in which American audiences of the nineteenth and early twentieth century often encountered new music for the first time. Songwriters were therefore often employed in the theater, whether directly or indirectly. Some were engaged to write for a specific production; others simply used the stage as a marketplace—a place where they could sell their wares, song by song. After all, it was filled with theatrical producers, directors, and performers looking for hit songs.

As a result, the American stage played a significant role in shaping American popular music throughout the nineteenth and the first half of the twentieth century. Indeed, even media such as recordings, films, and radio—all of which would eventually overtake the theater as preferred ways to popularize new songs—initially took a back seat to the stage, complementing it rather than functioning as a replacement. It was not until the 1930s that these media—along with television in the 1950s—began to displace the theater from its previously dominant role in shaping and disseminating American popular music.

The history of the American stage is therefore extremely important to the American Songbook. In particular, thanks to what transpired in musical theater in the first half of the twentieth century, Broadway became an incubator for the kind of songwriting found in this collection. The proliferation of musical comedy in late 1910s and 1920s marked the first important shift, one that ultimately led to the development of the popular standard as a song type.

REVUE VS. MUSICAL COMEDY

In 1914, Jerome Kern wrote a song called "They Didn't Believe Me" for a British musical comedy entitled *The Girl from Utah* when it was transplanted to New York. In his account of Kern's life and music, Gerald Bordman speaks to the historical significance of the song. "In interviews for this book," he writes, "few comments have come up as often as the remark that this great song established the popular musical comedy number as it was to remain for the next half-century." The reason, he says, is that unlike most songs before it, "They Didn't Believe Me" is "pristine and timeless."

Bordman's characterization of "They Didn't Believe Me" situates it firmly within the American Songbook, an early—and perhaps even the first—example of what would become the popular standard. Of course, Kern would go on to write more songs with these qualities, but he would also produce songs of a more ephemeral nature. Just two years later, for instance, he collaborated with lyricist Gene Buck for the *Ziegfeld Follies of 1916*. One of their songs was "My Lady of the Nile," part of a musical travesty on William Shakespeare's *Antony and Cleopatra* situated early in the revue. Notably, Buck's lyrics—as suggested by his title—allude to both the setting and the characters of Shakespeare's play. Still, the song is written in such a way that it could be used in allegorical fashion—or, with a couple of word substitutions, be reworked to suit other characters in love. After all, there are certainly universal sentiments in the song. The song did not live beyond its premiere, however, largely because its expressive nature was so strongly influenced by and suited to the Follies. Buck's lyrics present the female character in an idealized manner; her beauty is emphasized to the point of fantasy. This kind of imagery, common to many Follies songs, corresponds to the way in which women of the chorus were displayed on stage in these revues. Kern expresses the same thing musically. As Bordman suggests, he provided "a chorus sufficiently languid to allow a parade of Ziegfeld beauties," one that is "pleasant but trite."

This is quite different from what Kern wrote in "They Didn't Believe Me" two years earlier. Its protagonist also speaks about feminine beauty but in a decidedly more realistic and even ironic way. He, too, describes the object of his affection in glowing terms. In the words of lyricist Herbert Reynolds, her various attributes—lips, eyes, cheeks, and hair—"are in a class beyond compare." But this protagonist also emphasizes that her interest in him is difficult to grasp—for both him and his friends. "They'll never believe me," he says, that someone like her could actually choose someone like him. This response balances his romantic vision with realism and self-doubt. Such nuance makes the song less sentimental and ultimately more human. And, of course, Kern echoes this with more evocative music. His melody is rich and full, a beautiful balance of fluid movement, a few unexpected twists and leaps, and just enough repetition to make it feel whole.

To be sure, Kern's collaboration with Gene Buck is undoubtedly responsible for much of the differences between these two songs. Buck was in many ways the man behind Florenz Ziegfeld, executing much of what made these revues what they were—stunning, star-studded shows. As such, he wrote just the kind of lyrics needed for the Follies—ones that would not detract from the visual spectacles on stage. Kern could only respond to this with what we might think of as musical wallpaper. It is not unattractive, but neither is it an interesting work of art. It is something to be heard but not really noticed.

As such, it was the Follies themselves that shaped what Kern produced for them. As important as songs were to these and other spectacular revues of the period, the genre relied primarily on either this kind of musical wallpaper or on musical novelty. Songs that were topical, humorous, or quaint were also germane to the revue, but they were

even more limited in their ability to transcend this context. If they did
not rely on current events for their relevance, they relied on the specific
talents of an individual performer or the type of skit in which they were
used. As such, the revue did not foster the kind of songs Kern excelled
at writing—songs that were dramatically useful, universally meaningful,
and musically compelling. For that, he would need what *The Girl from
Utah* had provided—the backdrop of musical comedy.

American musical comedy was created in large part by recent immigrants to the country, those who were collectively interested in distinguishing their work from the numerous European imports seen by
Broadway patrons in the first two decades of the twentieth century.
Even so, they inevitably drew inspiration from these sources in some
ways—such as the role of everyday characters in the comic opera tradition. In the vein of Mozart's *The Marriage of Figaro*, for instance,
musical comedies typically feature plots involving ordinary men and
women—albeit Americans rather than Europeans—who, in the process
of falling in love, encounter any number of humorous complications.
For the sake of comedy, these complications were often far-fetched and
even ridiculous. The characters—and, more importantly, their feelings—were often remarkably human, however. As such, these shows
needed songs showcasing the full range of emotions experienced in
response to love. They needed songs about falling in love, unrequited
love, and lost love. They needed songs about romantic foibles and conflicts as well as celebrations. In some cases, they even needed songs
about other kinds of love, such as the love between parents and children or the love of something other than another person. The love of
music or dance, for instance, surfaces as a theme in a number of musical comedies. In short, musical comedies called for a broad range of
love songs—especially ones that were far more realistic in their expression than the sentimental numbers and sexually suggestive selections
most often found in revues and vaudeville.

And so, as musical comedies became increasingly popular on Broadway in the late 1910s and 1920s, the demand for such love songs
boomed. Revues remained, of course, but they gradually became less
dominant as more musical comedies were produced. Revues also
changed. It became increasingly difficult—and eventually impossible—
to produce spectacular revues on the scale of the Ziegfeld Follies. The
costs involved were becoming prohibitive, and it was becoming increas-

ingly difficult to improve upon earlier shows. As a result, the revues of the 1930s—and even a handful of revues of the 1920s—were far less visually oriented and far more like musical comedy in their style. They retained the basic structure and comic nature of the revue, but they lost their glamour and sentimentality.

JEROME KERN AND MUSICAL COMEDY

Jerome Kern was among the earliest to enjoy the beginning stages of this shift. Shortly after he wrote "They Didn't Believe Me" for *The Girl from Utah*, he collaborated with Guy Bolton on the first of a series of musical comedies staged at the recently built Princess Theater. The small size of the Princess demanded a more intimate kind of production—something very different from lavish revues such as the Ziegfeld Follies. Kern and Bolton responded to this by adapting a British play by Paul Rubens into a musical comedy designed for a New York audience. Under the new title *Nobody Home*, they crafted a show about an unlikely romance between a song-and-dance man and a wealthy socialite. Although it did not produce any of the Kern songs usually considered part of the American Songbook, it set the stage—quite literally—for the kind of shows that would foster such numbers. In fact, *Oh, Boy!*, which Kern and Bolton wrote along with P. G. Wodehouse for the Princess in 1917, offered audiences their first hearing of "Till the Clouds Roll By"—a song that proved so synonymous with Kern by the end of his career that it was used as the title for a 1946 fictionalized film about his life and work.

In 1920, Kern wrote music for another landmark musical comedy showcasing the talents of Marilyn Miller—a dancer who had risen to Broadway fame in the *Ziegfeld Follies of 1919* the previous year. Known simply as *Sally*, the show tells the story of a young girl who rises from humble beginnings as an orphan and dishwasher to become a celebrated Broadway dancer—and who also finds true love along the way to stardom. It was for this context that Kern collaborated with B. G. De-Sylva to write "Look for the Silver Lining," a song that exemplifies all the traits of the American Songbook and, like "Till the Clouds Roll By," demonstrates how musical comedy helped foster these traits.

In each of these songs, Kern and the lyricists with whom he collaborated make the most of the verse and chorus structure. The verses allude to specific contextual elements of the story, enabling the singers to logically introduce them into the plot. They also feature music that is more like dialogue; their melodies are not very repetitive and follow a less-formulaic phrase pattern. Conversely, the choruses convey emotions and broader themes related to but not specific to the story. Musically, they are more predictable and memorable, with clear phrases and repeated contours.

In "Till the Clouds Roll By," for instance, the verse speaks directly to the situation in the story of *Oh, Boy!* George is about to leave his home so that Jackie, who is pretending to be his wife in order to evade the police, can spend the night there in respectable fashion. As such, Jackie uses her lines to explain her situation further and to express regret that George has to leave when it is starting to rain; George then reassures her, noting that he would rather be wet than improper. Kern sets this to a meandering melody with only brief moments of repetition. The chorus is an extension of this introduction, of course, but it is far more general in its applicability and more structured in its musical style. The lyrics become metaphorical, referring not simply to the actual rain and clouds but also to the stormy situation in which Jackie and George find themselves. As such, the song becomes universal, conveying a message about waiting for a brighter day to come. Kern anchors this sentiment with even melodic phrases as well as more expanded use of repetition.

Similarly, in the verse of "Look for the Silver Lining," the leading character, Sally, sings about washing dishes. Thanks to some encouragement from the wealthy and sophisticated Blair Farquar, she determines to use this daily task in order to dream about what might be. Kern sets their lyrics with even yet distinct phrases, giving it a sense of continual movement rather than the structure of repetition and contrast. In the chorus, Sally and Blair sing in more general terms about embracing a positive outlook on life. For this, Kern follows an easily audible pattern, albeit one that features less repetition than might be considered typical. Because the entire structure is repeated, however, the melody as a whole becomes memorable.

Of course, this explains why verses from these and other standards are often omitted from recordings and other nontheatrical performances. Unlike the choruses, they are often limited in their applicability because they were written to serve a specific situation. Even in cases where the lyrics are less restrictive, the less-formulaic approach to melodic writing in the verse makes them more difficult to remember. They are no less interesting than the choruses, but they are less catchy.

Oddly enough, it was the man who had discovered Marilyn Miller and launched the widespread popularity of the spectacular revue, none other than Florenz Ziegfeld, who produced *Sally*. His involvement is noteworthy, for he was the one who hired Kern to write the songs for the show. This suggests that he may have understood more about music than is often suggested—not in technical or theoretical terms but in theatrical and entrepreneurial ones. With his status in the Broadway community, he could have asked anyone to write songs for this venture into musical comedy. He could have hired the team of Gene Buck and Dave Stamper, who had contributed numerous songs to the Follies in recent years. Or he could have hired Irving Berlin, who had written a number of hit selections for the *Ziegfeld Follies of 1919*. And yet, he thought Jerome Kern, whose songs had not done very well in the Follies, was the right man for this job. He seems to have understood that a musical comedy required something different in musical terms than his topical and visually oriented revues.

THE GERSHWINS AND MUSICAL COMEDY

Like Jerome Kern, George Gershwin wrote for both revues and musical comedies in the early stages of his career. And, like Kern, Gershwin also produced most of his enduring hits in the realm of musical comedy. He worked regularly on a series of revues known as *George White's Scandals* in the early 1920s, for which he wrote "I'll Build a Stairway to Paradise" (1922) and "Somebody Loves Me" (1924). But these are the only standards to emerge from the much larger repertoire Gershwin wrote for these shows. By contrast, the musical comedy *Lady, Be Good!* (1924) introduced "Fascinating Rhythm," "Oh, Lady Be Good!" and "Little Jazz Bird." All of these have enjoyed long lives as popular standards.

In his time-honored biography of Gershwin, Edward Jablonski describes the plot of *Lady, Be Good!* as "convoluted and rarely logical." Even so, it provided the kind of backdrop that fostered songs with timeless qualities. One reason for this may well be that *Lady, Be Good!*, like the shows Kern wrote for the Princess, was crafted by Guy Bolton—in this case with another collaborator, Fred Thompson. Bolton's work at the Princess had shown that he understood the importance of creating good characters; what happened to them did not matter as much. With Fred and Adele Astaire set to appear in the leading roles, Bolton and Thompson had even more going for them—not to mention Ira Gershwin, who would finally begin working regularly with his brother for the production.

When we look at the songs the Gershwins wrote for *Lady, Be Good!*, it becomes easy to see how their original purpose actually helped them transcend it. For example, both "Fascinating Rhythm" and "Little Jazz Bird" are performed by the character Jeff White (originally portrayed by Cliff "Ukulele Ike" Edwards), a musical entertainer. He sings them at parties attended by Dick and Susie Trevor (originally played by Fred and Adele Astaire), who are, like their real-life counterparts, a brother-and-sister dance team. Because these songs are performed as entertainment in this way, their music and lyrics do not need to have any relationship to the plot or the characters. Of course, the Gershwins' choice to make music itself the subject of both songs makes them even more appropriate for the characters in *Lady, Be Good*—and even more appealing to listeners far removed from the theater. "Fascinating Rhythm" is a song about the irresistible and unrelenting appeal of rhythm, a topic that hardly needed translation between the stage and the dance floor—especially since George's music conveys the message as much as Ira's lyrics. Similarly, "Little Jazz Bird" is a cleverly colloquial statement about the appeal of jazz, which resonated just as easily with almost anyone living in the 1920s—not to mention many others in subsequent generations.

The Gershwin brothers produced a number of hit songs that premiered in musical comedies over the next few years, including selections for *Oh, Kay!* and *Funny Face*—produced by the team behind *Lady, Be Good!*, Alex Aarons and Vinton Freedley—as well as those for the Ziegfeld musical comedies *Rosalie* and *Show Girl*. Then, in 1930, they composed a list of hits for *Girl Crazy*—another Aarons and Freedley vehicle that brought fame to both Ethel Merman and Ginger Rogers. This one show introduced "Bidin' My Time," "But Not for Me," "Could You Use Me," "Embraceable You," and "I Got Rhythm"—not to mention a number of other, somewhat less-familiar titles in the Gershwin catalog.

That a single show could include such a substantial list of songs that were widely enjoyed at the time and remain familiar today speaks volumes about the compatibility of musical comedy and the popular standard. The genre had left behind over-the-top sentimentality and topical humor in favor of songs that expressed the desires of everyday characters. As a result, these songs moved easily from the stage into the homes of millions of people who shared those desires.

THE SPECIAL CASE OF IRVING BERLIN

As Jeffrey Magee writes in his insightful study of Irving Berlin and American musical theater, Berlin "sustained a belief in the integrity of individual songs to be able to stand alone outside of whatever original theatrical context for which they may have been conceived." With this kind of philosophy, it is easy to understand why so many Berlin songs have become part of the American Songbook—not to mention why he valued the opinion of the masses, why his most popular songs were also his favorites, and why he proved to be an astute businessman as well as a songwriter. It may also explain why his contributions have their origins more equally distributed between musical comedies and revues—why, as in so many other cases, he is the exception that proves the rule. For example, "Blue Skies" may have been introduced in a musical comedy in 1926, but "A Pretty Girl Is Like a Melody" and "Mandy" were first heard in the most noteworthy revue of the previous decade—the *Ziegfeld Follies of 1919*.

Berlin had a long history with Ziegfeld, sporadically contributing songs to the Follies between 1911 and 1918. In 1919, however, he wrote a significant portion of the show—something he would do again in the *Ziegfeld Follies of 1927*. Some of these songs, such as the Prohibition commentary "You Cannot Make Your Shimmy Shake on Tea," were entirely ephemeral—and were obviously meant to be. With "A Pretty Girl" and "Mandy," however, he strove for and accomplished something else. These songs demonstrate what Magee describes as Berlin's "deft ability to both address his immediate audience and write songs generally enough to endure beyond the contemporary moment."

This is especially noteworthy in the case of "A Pretty Girl," for it epito-mized the style and essence of the Follies to such an extent that it became the musical number that symbolized the entire series—the best of all the musical tributes to the Ziegfeld Girl. And, in addition to this thematic significance, it was crafted for the Follies with remarkable specificity. Berlin wrote the song to fit a particular need. Ziegfeld wanted to present several Follies dancers in costumes that represented familiar classical melodies, and he needed a musical introduction for the sequence. Berlin provided the perfect simile in the form of a song.

Despite all of this, "A Pretty Girl" has still managed to enjoy a signif-icant life beyond its original purpose—not only in pop-culture phenom-ena indebted to the Follies, such as film musicals and beauty pageants, but also in performances further removed from the theater. The reason for this, of course, is that it has the kind of tuneful melody and universal ideas found in so many standards. That Berlin could write such a stan-dard for such a specific purpose attests to his special talents as a song-writer. It also demonstrates his aforementioned belief in writing songs designed for appeal outside a particular theatrical context.

Over time, Berlin's contributions to the revue itself helped make it a more suitable vehicle for songs with timeless qualities. This process began between 1921 and 1924, when he partnered with Sam Harris to produce the *Music Box Revues*. With these shows, Berlin strove for something different than the spectacular revues popularized by Zieg-feld and his competitors—something that privileged the origins of the revue as social satire and commentary and used music as a cohesive element rather than a backdrop or comic tool. He continued to experi-ment with this to some extent on the *Ziegfeld Follies of 1927*, though Ziegfeld's omnipresence did not enable him to enjoy the same creative control he had enjoyed with the *Music Box Revues*. By 1933, however, he was able to collaborate with Moss Hart on a revue that departed further from the Ziegfeld model—especially with respect to music. *As Thousands Cheer* is noteworthy for a number of reasons, one of which is that it introduced an unusual number of Berlin standards including "Easter Parade" and "Heat Wave." This would hardly have happened without Berlin's craftsmanship—not only as a songwriter but also as a showman.

MUSICAL COMEDY OVER TIME

Irving Berlin was unusual in his ability to craft songs with timeless qualities regardless of the dramatic context. Most of his contemporaries found musical comedy a more suitable vehicle for these kinds of songs. As musical comedies continued to grow in popularity, so did the number of standards that emerged from them. What makes this all the more interesting is that most of these early musical comedies have not enjoyed anything like the life of the songs contained in them. The reason, of course, is that their stories were not especially noteworthy. This is the ironic thing about them. Because they featured true-to-life characters, they fostered timeless love songs, but they were rarely timeless themselves. This would change, however, beginning with *Show Boat* in 1927.

When he decided to make a musical version of the Edna Ferber novel *Show Boat*, Florenz Ziegfeld once again turned to Jerome Kern to write the songs. Kern came through with flying colors, of course, producing a score that richly and beautifully contributes to the stories of the men and women aboard the *Cotton Blossom* riverboat. It abounds with familiar and beloved titles, including "Can't Help Lovin' That Man," "Ol' Man River," "Make Believe," and "You Are Love." But while these songs have enjoyed a life beyond the original production, its subsequent film versions, and its numerous stage revivals, they do bear a stronger connection to their original context than most of the standards written for earlier musical comedies. The reason for this is that even though they convey universal ideas and have the kind of musical tunefulness germane to the standard, they also have a more pronounced dramatic purpose in their original context. They help tell the story of *Show Boat*, something few if any songs had actually accomplished in earlier American stage shows. Kern had experimented with the concept in his shows at the Princess, but he took a much bigger leap forward with *Show Boat*. For this latest show, he produced melodies related to one another and used them for dramatic purposes—both when sung and when played by the accompanying orchestra. His collaborator, Oscar Hammerstein II, wrote lyrics that not only conveyed universally felt emotions but also raised issues about humanity and American culture.

This kind of musical writing would become increasingly common on Broadway in the coming decades, especially as composers and lyricists also emulated *Show Boat* in another key way—the use of a more sophisticated plot. Stephen Banfield, in his study of the Broadway musical, refers to this even more simply—and perhaps even more aptly—as the use of a "better book." After all, *Show Boat* is not really musical comedy—at least as the genre existed prior to the 1930s. Its story is neither a lighthearted romance nor a farce but an epic tale, and its characters experience not only genuine emotions but also genuine struggles—including addiction, abandonment, oppression, and more. As such, it set the stage for subsequent musical shows touching on more serious issues, including *Oklahoma!*, *South Pacific*, and others written by the team of Richard Rodgers and Oscar Hammerstein.

Notably, these shows also have the same kind of relationship with the American Songbook as does *Show Boat*. Their songs—such as "Oh, What a Beautiful Morning" and "There is Nothing Like a Dame"—have a certain currency beyond the theater, but most listeners still associate them with the productions for which they were written. In this respect, this more-developed kind of musical comedy was somewhat less conducive to the creation of truly popular standards—ones that stand apart from any particular context. Over time, this would make Broadway more innovative in theatrical terms but also less influential in American popular culture as a whole—especially popular music culture.

This shift was gradual, of course, and many musical shows of the 1940s and 1950s continued to produce songs in much the same style as popular standards of earlier years. Many listeners would even consider at least some of these to be part of the American Songbook, and justifiably so. Still, it is important to understand that as music became more integrated into the stories of Broadway shows, these shows became less capable of launching popular songs. They simply were not structured to do so.

The period in which the popular standard and the Broadway musical proved so compatible is therefore relatively small—albeit a period with fluid boundaries at both the beginning and the end. The birth of the musical film, however, would help extend this period and greatly expand the repertoire of the American Songbook. As Broadway became an arena for musical and dramatic innovation, Hollywood became a haven for the standard.

4

THE AMERICAN SONGBOOK ON SCREEN

The film musical proved to be an ideal vehicle for the American Song-book—in part because so many of the creative talents who had fostered the development of these songs on Broadway heard the call of Holly-wood by the early 1930s. In particular, songwriters such as Irving Ber-lin, Jerome Kern, and the Gershwin brothers now found a home for their songs on screen—and they spent most of the 1930s working on both coasts as a result. In some cases, songs previously introduced on Broadway were rendered in this new format. A year after its Broadway introduction, for instance, Irving Berlin's "Blue Skies" became part of the landmark film *The Jazz Singer*. Two years later, Jerome Kern's "Look for the Silver Lining" reached the other coast with the 1929 film version of *Sally*, in which Marilyn Miller reprised her stage role. Then, as film became more popular, new songs and new musical comedies were written for the medium. Both Berlin and Kern would be part of this. In fact, the films of Fred Astaire and Ginger Rogers proved an especially important showcase for their work in the 1930s, with songs such as Berlin's "Cheek to Cheek" and "Isn't It a Lovely Day (To Be Caught in the Rain)" appearing in *Top Hat* (1935) and Kern's "Smoke Gets in Your Eyes" and "I Won't Dance" heard in *Roberta* (1935).

To be sure, there were important and influential songwriters who worked in Hollywood without any significant background on Broadway. These include people like Harry Warren, Arthur Freed, and Johnny Mercer. But even though their musical influences and experience be-gan elsewhere, they entered a world that had ultimately precipitated from the Broadway stage. Their songs certainly illustrate the unique musical fingerprints of their creators, from the richly southern flavor of Johnny Mercer's lyrics to the comical vaudevillian sensibilities of Arthur Freed. But they also fit the basic framework of the popular standard as it had been developed and nurtured on the Great White Way.

Hollywood thus became an extension of Broadway and ultimately an even more important incubator for the popular standard. For one thing, the national distribution of film meant a much larger audience than any theatrical production could gain—both immediately and in the long haul. The preserved nature of film has enabled it to play an immeasurably important and uniquely nostalgic role in the widespread familiarity of the American Songbook in more recent years. More importantly, though, film provided a place for the standard to grow and develop. It would continue to do so even as fewer and fewer new standards were being written. This happened because film could—and gradually did—incorporate songs in far less presentational ways. To be sure, early film musicals followed the Broadway model of the 1920s and therefore nurtured the popular standard in much the same way as their stage counterparts. Over time, however, film characters started to sing for their own enjoyment rather than for an audience within the story. Or they might listen to a song on the radio or from a record player, making film audiences privy to their reactions as they hear the words and music. These and other dramatic roles for song gave the standard, with its broadly applicable design, a place to thrive—and, perhaps more importantly, to endure.

Four standards performed on film between the 1930s and the 1960s can collectively illustrate the gradual move from stage-like song performances to characters singing in more casual, personal, and ordinary ways. Film renderings of these songs show how, during this period, filmmakers and songwriters expanded the ways in which singing could be contextualized on screen. Subsequent use of these songs on film further demonstrates how the standard, due to its inherent adaptability, helped make this shift possible, such that standards initially used in largely performative ways have been adapted to more natural settings in more recent films. These examples represent how the standard has been used on film over time; from the spectacular to the simple, they show the range of how the standard and the movie screen have shaped and been shaped by one another.

STEP ONE: "YOU'RE GETTING TO BE A HABIT WITH ME"

As was the case on Broadway in the 1920s, film writers and directors in the early years often used the entertainment industry as a backdrop for their love stories. The reason for this was both simple and practical: characters who were themselves entertainers had more reason to burst into song and dance than most others. Notably, this was true not only for moments when such characters were actually performing in a "show within the show" but also at other times. These were men and women who, by virtue of their profession, could start singing even in contexts that were not inherently musical without other characters in the story—or indeed the audience watching them—finding it strange.

To be sure, approaches to the so-called backstage musical varied quite a bit. The films of Fred Astaire and Ginger Rogers, for instance, involve characters who earn their living through song and dance. Many of their musical numbers, however, actually transpire in everyday life. Their ability to perform stems from their profession, but their desire to perform is largely personal. Alternatively, choreographer Busby Berkeley admired the spectacle that had been germane to the Broadway revue. As such, his films emphasize the connection between the visual and the musical more than the connection between song and character or song and plot. In this sense, many of his films are as much "onstage musicals" as they are "backstage musicals." He clearly favors what his characters do in their professional lives more than what transpires behind the scenes.

Accordingly, the films of Busby Berkeley include some of the most performative song renderings in Hollywood history, songs that are overtly performed within their dramatic context—often lavishly so. One such example is "You're Getting to Be a Habit with Me." The song, with music by Harry Warren and lyrics by Al Dubin, is one of several production numbers featured in the landmark film *42nd Street* (1933). It is sung by the character of Dorothy Brock (played by Bebe Daniels), who is shown rehearsing the number for her upcoming show. The film audience not only sees Brock and the male performers who accompany her on stage; they are also able to witness the other members of the cast waiting in the wings for their next cue as well as the members of the orchestra accompanying her.

The lyrics of "You're Getting to Be a Habit with Me" embody the essence of the standard, describing the increased longing that often develops as a person falls in love. Set to a tuneful, catchy melody, such a song would be easily extractable from any film context. In this case, however, it is not even relevant to the plot of the film. It is used purely as a performance number; Dorothy Brock even sings about devotion to one man while dancing with several—perhaps an attempt at irony but without anything else in the story to support it. As such, the song's expression of romantic engagement is not represented with any degree of realism whatsoever. Instead, it is dramatically disconnected except as a showcase of Brock's talent and a rehearsal number needed to move the production process forward.

Of course, the performance is still a beautiful one, and it obviously introduced the song to its original film audience. Such an approach is limiting, however, because it requires a plot in which performing is germane. As time would show, only so many films of this type could be successful—especially as film became less of a novelty and audience expectations grew. Filmmakers gradually began to draw more heavily on the universal expression of the standard and its greater dramatic flexibility, strengthening and expanding the relationship between the American Songbook and the silver screen.

STEP TWO: "THE WAY YOU LOOK TONIGHT"

Fred Astaire had an extensive and successful career on stage before making the transition to film. This may explain, at least in part, why his film work seems like a continuation of what had transpired on Broadway in the previous decade, especially with respect to how songs are situated within the stories he helps tell. Though most of his films still use the entertainment industry as a backdrop in some way, he rarely sings—or dances, for that matter—in a purely presentational manner, as Bebe Daniels does in *42nd Street*. Instead, most of his singing occurs in more ordinary circumstances.

In some cases, such as his rendition of Irving Berlin's "Isn't This a Lovely Day (To Be Caught in the Rain)" in *Top Hat* (1935), the song itself provides the premise. Here, Astaire and Ginger Rogers enjoy a sheltered dance in and around a gazebo while waiting out a rain shower.

They are not performing but simply dancing together. To be sure, the professional quality of the number and its over-the-top romanticism might make it seem far-fetched—especially for contemporary audiences. In dramatic terms, however, it represents a departure from the need for a show within the show.

The same is true for "The Way You Look Tonight," which Astaire sings to Rogers in *Swing Time* (1936). The scene involving the song is contrived but brilliantly so. Astaire's character, "Lucky" Garnett, is trying to win favor with Rogers's character, Penny Carroll. When she won't open the door to him, he sits down at a conveniently placed piano nearby and begins to serenade her. Penny is easily swayed by the melody, so much so that she forgets what she is doing—washing her hair—and approaches him at the piano with a sudsy head and a towel draped around her neck. Lucky keeps singing without looking at her, retaining whatever image lies in his mind at the moment. But when he finishes, he turns toward her and is a bit surprised by what he sees. Penny then looks in the mirror and runs away embarrassed.

Obviously, the filmmakers were striving for irony here, and yet the song remains genuinely romantic and honest at the same time. This is possible in large part because Astaire's singing moves away from a solely performative mode and toward something else. He is performing, in a sense, but only for an audience of one—the woman he loves. This makes the film audience privy to something far more personal, far more intimate than is the case for the backstage setting of *42nd Street* and other such films. Here, the emotions are real. Some aspects of the scene, like the ready availability of a sparkling black piano and the beautiful clothes worn by Astaire and Rogers, are designed to create a Hollywood fantasy. The essential circumstance, however, is perfectly ordinary. Nearly every man has been rejected, nearly every man has tried to regain affection through some sort of romantic gesture, and nearly every woman has responded favorably to such attempts.

The film camera adds to the intimacy of the scene. It brings the film audience closer to the characters, enabling them to see facial expressions with far greater clarity than could ever be possible on stage. In this particular case, it allows Astaire's singing to resonate especially well with his audience. Those watching can easily imagine the image of Penny he sees in his mind as he sings and recognize that, despite his expected surprise at seeing her differently, her appearance is actually more memorable and more endearing than what he originally had in his mind. Of course, the camera also captures Penny's response to Lucky with exceptional clarity. This is true not only because the camera can provide the audience with an equally close-up view of her face but also because it can alternate between the two characters. Director George Stevens chooses his moments to focus on each character carefully, and the audience is therefore privy to how Penny's emotions unfold throughout the song.

This results in a song performance that is as beautifully constructed as those of Busby Berkeley, but that is far more communicative and relatable. To be sure, it still enables the audience to enjoy the talents of Astaire and Rogers, but it also encourages them to see Lucky and Penny as characters not all that different from themselves. For this to happen, of course, the song needs to have the qualities of a standard—and "The Way You Look Tonight" does. Dorothy Fields's lyrics speak to universal feelings, ones that are so commonly felt that the song has become enormously popular for wedding dances—an occasion when brides and grooms are typically looking especially memorable. Jerome Kern's simple yet unique melody carries this thought beautifully—and it is memorable in its own right. As such, it was perfectly suited to its original film context and to being enjoyed in others as well.

STEP THREE: "SINGIN' IN THE RAIN"

Singin' in the Rain is one the most beloved film musicals ever made. Of course, it continues the tradition of the backstage musical with a provocative twist; its entertainment backdrop is the advent of sound film. This setting, created by writers Betty Comden and Adolph Green, facilitated a great deal of industry-related humor and made the film chronologically suited to the songs it was scheduled to include—a collection of tunes authored by lyricist Arthur Freed and composer Nacio Herb Brown in the 1920s and early 1930s. Freed and Brown had written these songs while working for MGM, several of which were used in films such as *The Broadway Melody* (1929) and *Hollywood Revue* (1929). The team had clearly been influenced by the musical evolution of the standard. Their songs, while perhaps less innovative than some other selections in the American Songbook, possess everything it takes to make a good standard. They speak to universal themes like love and loss, they have tuneful melodies that are easily remembered, and they are able to retain their essence in various manifestations. As such, they had the potential to work in a wide range of dramatic situations. In 1929, however, they were just production numbers for star performers; filmmakers were far more interested in the technological capabilities of sound film than in how they could use music to tell stories. By 1952, however, Hollywood had changed.

Arthur Freed had gone on to pursue an enormously successful career at MGM—not as a songwriter but as a producer. He, along with a core group of directors, choreographers, and stars known as the "Freed Unit," played an important role in making many of the studio's most enduringly popular musicals, including *The Wizard of Oz*, *Meet Me in St. Louis*, *Easter Parade*, *An American in Paris*, and *Singin' in the Rain*. Not surprisingly, it was Freed who charged Comden and Green to write a screenplay around his songs—possibly because he just wanted to bring them back into the public ear, but perhaps because he felt they could be used in more dramatically interesting ways than had previously been the case. After all, "Singin' in the Rain" did become popular as a hit song in 1929, but the rendition seen in *Hollywood Revue* was little more than a visual spectacle set to music.

Gene Kelly's version of the song, on the other hand, is among the most familiar and most adored song performances ever captured on screen. It is a masterpiece of choreography, not only because it is so beautifully constructed as a dance sequence but also because it is so naturally integrated into the storytelling. It is not a production number, as one might expect for such a song in a film about show business. Instead, it is a personal expression of joy. Kelly's character, Don Lockwood, begins singing just because he wants to do so. He has no audience at all, except for a passing policeman who happens to see the last few steps of his routine. He is simply choosing to enjoy his life at a particularly happy moment—one in which he feels the promise of both professional success and romance. His circumstances are therefore a perfect match to Freed's upbeat lyrics and Brown's celebratory-sounding music. In fact, it is an excellent example of how the standard serves the film musical—and vice versa. Nothing about the song relates explicitly to the scene, yet its emotional expression is perfectly suited to Kelly's character at that moment. And Kelly's performance has kept a song that might otherwise have disappeared from popular culture so familiar that scores of people continue to hum, sing, or whistle bits of the song at happy moments in their everyday lives—perhaps especially when it happens to be raining.

Because Gene Kelly's routine is carefully choreographed and his dancing is so exceptional, some viewers might be reluctant to think of it as realistic in any way. But like Fred Astaire's rendition of "The Way You Look Tonight," the song has a very ordinary place in the story—a situation where almost anyone might consider singing. Audiences still recognize it as a staged musical performance, but they also experience it as something more than just a show. This might well be the reason "Singin' in the Rain" has enjoyed a more enduring status in American popular culture than most of the other songs in the film. "Broadway Melody," for instance, is entirely performative—part of a dream ballet sequence Kelly's character is busy developing for his upcoming film. The same is true for "All I Do Is Dream of You," the song that introduces Kathy as a chorus girl—a sharp cultural contrast to the serious actress she wants to be, but a role that endears her to the more humble Don Lockwood. Even "Would You," one of the romantic ballads of the film, is used both on screen and off screen. It does advance the budding romance between Don and Kathy but only tangentially; it also serves the film within the film. "Singin' in the Rain" thus stands out as a remarkably real moment in the film, one that foreshadows even more everyday singing and dancing in later films.

STEP FOUR: "MOON RIVER"

In his biography of Johnny Mercer, Philip Furia makes an astute observation about the songwriter's career. He describes Mercer's approach to writing lyrics as "refined concentration on the emotional mood of a melody," a process that was not especially conducive to the theater—at least as it existed by the 1930s and 1940s. He probably would have done well writing for musical comedy in the 1920s, Furia suggests, but the post–*Show Boat* era asked lyricists to think "not only about the music they were setting but about plot, character, and theatricality." Fortunately for Mercer, Hollywood—as well as the burgeoning recording industry—offered far more varied opportunities, and he enjoyed a successful career writing songs for a wide range of films and popular sing-ers. At times, he was asked to write for something more theatrical in nature, and he did adapt to some degree. Most of his best-known songs, however, were written for films that allowed him to rely more heavily on his natural instincts as a lyricist—instincts that prioritize the pairing of words and melody. Not coincidentally, of course, this approach is the very essence of the popular standard.

By the time Mercer collaborated with Henry Mancini on "Moon River" for the 1961 film *Breakfast at Tiffany's*, however, writing stan-dards was no longer common in the entertainment industry. Instead, songs were written with far more specificity, designed to serve a unique dramatic situation, a particular singer's voice, or a group of listeners. Still, Mercer embraced the songwriting technique that had served him well in the past and managed to create a timeless standard at a time when such a thing must have seemed difficult or even impossible. He took Mancini's melody, with its evocative contours and ethereal flavor, and turned it into an anthem of reminiscence—something ideally suited to the character of Holly Golightly that would also resonate with almost anyone watching her story unfold. This sense of universal human expe-rience is strengthened by the way in which they song is used in the film. Holly, famously portrayed by Audrey Hepburn, sings it very simply while sitting in her windowsill and accompanying herself on the guitar. It seems to be a melody she learned in childhood, and she sings it as she remembers the home she left behind before coming to New York City.

In short, the performance is anything but performative. There is no audience, except for Holly's upstairs neighbor, who opens his window and peers down the fire escape to learn more about this intriguing and forlorn young woman living beneath him. Moreover, Holly's voice is not presentational. Audrey Hepburn was capable of more performative singing; she had done it opposite Fred Astaire in *Funny Face*. As Holly, however, the filmmakers emphasized the naturalness of her voice—the way she could sound like an ordinary young woman. Of course, this choice lent itself exceptionally well to the story, helped popularize the song in an age when relatively few standards were still being crafted, and demonstrated that songs could be sung on film by virtually any kind of character.

THE LEGACY OF THE POPULAR STANDARD ON FILM

Everyday singing, like that done by Audrey Hepburn in *Breakfast at Tiffany's*, continues to feature prominently in contemporary films—especially in romantic comedies. And the American Songbook is one of the most widely used repertoires for this kind of music in film. In these cases, the goal is not to introduce a new song but rather to play upon its already established cultural meaning. Other iconic songs from the more recent past—including some that deviate stylistically from the popular standard—have also been used in this manner, yet these are often incorporated in some combination with their most familiar recorded version. Tom Cruise, for instance, sings along with Tom Petty's "Free Fallin'" when he hears it on the radio in *Jerry Maguire*. Because they are known primarily as music and lyrics, however, standards have retained a special kind of cultural resonance that enables them to be sung without any audible reference to a particular performance.

One example of this is when Dermot Mulroney's character sings "The Way You Look Tonight" in *My Best Friend's Wedding* (1997). Mulroney's character, Michael, is preparing to get married, and the film begins when he shares this news with his longtime female friend Julianne, played by Julia Roberts. Julianne has been denying her love for Michael for years, so much so that she doesn't even realize it until he announces his wedding. She then tries to muster up the courage to declare her feelings. One day, as the friends are discussing their past and future, Michael begins singing "The Way You Look Tonight"—a song that holds special meaning for them. The romantic overtones are obvious, of course; he even asks her to dance. As she moves into his arms and continues listening to the song, tears well up in her eyes. But still, she cannot bring herself to show them—or her true feelings—to Michael.

This use of "The Way You Look Tonight" is remarkable for several reasons. First, Michael sings it; he does not perform it. Although there are other people around, he is singing only to Julianne. Moreover, his voice is pleasant enough but not exceptional in any way—and that is part of what makes it believable for contemporary film audiences. The familiarity of the song also helps, of course, which is why a standard like "The Way You Look Tonight" is so ideal. It makes Michael's singing a romantic gesture but one that almost anyone could do. Second, the song carries a kind of dramatic weight that few others could. Everything about the original film version of the song—from the way in which Penny puts on the appearance of disinterest in Lucky to the mix of genuine affection and comical surprise in his response—holds special meaning here, as does the fact that "The Way You Look Tonight" is one of the most widely heard songs at contemporary weddings. As such, the song conveys far more than the literal meaning of the lyrics. Third, the scene demonstrates the place of "The Way You Look Tonight" and the American Songbook more generally in contemporary popular culture. Today's films often use music of the past to help situate the audience in the proper historical time frame. Here, however, there is no attempt to take the viewers back in time. Instead, the song is simply a classic—neither old nor new but timeless.

Another way in which the standard continues to permeate contemporary film is the use of recorded versions of this repertoire. In some cases, recordings are used entirely as nondiegetic music—something that enhances the experience of the audience but is not actually heard by the characters in the film. In others, though, they demonstrate a different kind of casual music experience; characters are seen putting on a record, turning on the radio, or perhaps hearing a song through a loud speaker. The first of these, in which the songs are used to contextualize the story, primarily demonstrates the historical place of the standard. The second, however, shows how standards have transcended the period of popular music history in which they were born—when recordings were only a small part of the popular music landscape—and established a continual presence in our contemporary world.

A good example of this is the use of Billie Holiday's recording of "The Very Thought of You" in the Mel Gibson film *Forever Young* (1992). The film opens when Gibson's character, Daniel, awakens after having been cryogenically frozen. He finds himself in unfamiliar surroundings, unable to make contact with anyone he once knew, and struggling to deal with certain realities of a new age. He does befriend a young boy named Nat and his mother, Claire, however, and they invite him to stay as a guest in their house until he sorts things out. Nat, who accidentally released Daniel from his frozen state, tries to help him understand modern technology. Claire, who learns about Daniel's story more gradually, offers other things—like compassion, hospitality, and a listening ear.

One day, Daniel comes across Claire's record collection and finds Billie Holiday's recording of "The Very Thought of You"—a song he used to enjoy with his girlfriend, Helen. He and Claire listen to it, and the music transports him back to the world he left. For Claire, it is a beautiful, nostalgic song with a kind of musical quality that is absent in more recent recordings. For Daniel, though, it is even more than this. It is a song that is so familiar and so meaningful that he ultimately cannot bear to hear it. The memories it evokes are simply too painful.

In a dramatic scenario like this, the use of a recording is obviously practical. There would be no contextual reason for anyone to sing. It is also especially poignant, however, for Daniel responds not only to the song but also to Billie Holiday's performance of it. It is her voice he used to hear as he held Helen in his arms, and it is that same voice—with all of its nuances—that he hears now. To be sure, another rendition of the same song would probably also elicit something in him, but to hear precisely the same version is especially powerful—even overwhelming. Moreover, the record as a physical object provides something unexpectedly familiar for Daniel. It is one of the few things he encounters that he actually recognizes and knows how to use. In a very literal way, it connects him with his new surroundings—which is both a blessing and a curse.

In these and in many other films, standards continue to play an important role. They still resonate in popular culture, both as representations of another time and as timeless melodies. As such, their relationship with film is particularly rich and strong. They obviously have a historical relationship, but they also have a contemporary one. In addition to new performances of this repertoire on film, audiences today can revisit earlier ones in a way that actually creates currency. Iconic images from these films continue to permeate the landscape of American popular culture, enabling younger generations to experience them not simply as artifacts but as an integral part of their own experience.

5

JAZZ AND THE AMERICAN SONGBOOK

As jazz moved into the mainstream in the 1920s, it became one of the most influential forces in American popular culture. It shaped all kinds of things, from the way people danced to the way they talked and the books they read. In an era marked by economic vitality, postwar confidence, and largely ineffective Prohibition laws, it is little wonder that jazz became a symbol of freedom in all its forms—physical, social, and political.

Jazz also shaped other kinds of music—often to such an extent that the boundaries between them become blurry. Some musicians made a conscious effort to capitalize on the craze for all things jazz, using it more as a marketing tool or a novelty than as a true artistic influence. Many, though, simply worked and collaborated with their fellow musicians in the musical richness of the period without regard to genre or category. For example, swing music giants Benny Goodman, Gene Krupa, Glenn Miller, Jimmy Dorsey, and Jack Teagarden all played in the orchestras that accompanied the Gershwin shows *Strike Up the Band* and *Girl Crazy* in 1930—on some occasions conducted by none other than the composer. This is hardly an exceptional circumstance, but the interaction of such key figures at this particular time and in this particular way points to how closely jazz and popular song would be intertwined by the 1930s.

This world of musical exchange and experimentation is made all the more rich—as well as more complicated—by the fact that jazz defies an easy definition. To be sure, it is a musical style rooted in African

American folk expression, which means that it frequently includes such techniques as sliding into and away from pitches, call and response, syncopation, and a mixture of major and minor modes—many of those things songwriters on Broadway found so appealing and useful in their own creative palette. Improvisation is also a key element of the genre, with approaches ranging from the loose but recognizable interpretation of a familiar melody to the generation of entirely new melodic ideas over a familiar accompaniment—or, in its most radical version of free jazz, the production of new melodic ideas without any attention to other dimensions of the musical context. And yet, these elements don't always make jazz—and not just in more recent jazz history, as stylistic variety within the genre has exploded. Even in its developing years, these jazz techniques could be heard in a wide variety of songs, some of which were identified as jazz and some of which were identified as popular. In fact, the race of the performer had a great deal more to do with how songs were labeled and marketed at this time than did the actual sound and substance of the music and lyrics. This explains why we have terms like "jazz standard" and "popular standard" even though, with a few notable exceptions, they do not really delineate different repertoires. Instead, they describe a common repertoire that is utilized by artists in what are now commonly identified as two different genres.

These fluid boundaries did two remarkable things for the American Songbook. First, they expanded its audience even further. Broadway had helped foster songs with appeal beyond the stage, and Hollywood had brought such songs to audiences across the country. Jazz, however, made this repertoire relevant for thousands of listeners who were further removed from mainstream America. As jazz artists performed these songs and contributed their own compositions, the American Songbook came to be as familiar to jazz fans as anyone else—and jazz had a special appeal with two groups who might not otherwise have encountered the American Songbook in such a meaningful way: African Americans and the French. Second, they made the popular standard an arena for musical experimentation. The interpretive freedom of jazz became germane to the popular standard as well, resulting in an unusually wide range of performance styles by both singers and instrumentalists. Without a connection to jazz, the American Songbook would probably be more dated stylistically, its universal and timeless qualities overshadowed at least in part by a rather homogenized performance history dominated by Broadway and film stars. Instead, though, jazz musicians have offered far more varied versions of the repertoire—and even performers based in these disciplines have had the opportunity to be shaped by jazz.

Of course, it remains true that certain standards have been more heavily shaped by jazz than others—both in their genesis and composition and in their performance history. Many songs are good examples of how jazz and popular music were interacting in the 1930s and 1940s and how their relationship has played out over time, but some illustrate the connection in especially poignant ways. Three songs in particular show the immense cultural resonance of both the standard and jazz, especially when operating in the same musical sphere. The first, "It Don't Mean a Thing If It Ain't Got That Swing," shows the contributions of jazz-based songwriters to the American Songbook as a repertoire, including how those contributions led other jazz musicians to explore the repertoire as a whole. The second, "April in Paris," demonstrates the full scope of jazz as an influence on the American Songbook—from its inherent musical qualities to its widespread and varied interpretations by jazz artists—even in a song that has equally significant connections to stage and screen. The third, "Body and Soul," is perhaps the quintessential jazz standard, one that is so deeply entrenched in the world of jazz that it almost seems distinct from the American Songbook—yet it ultimately illustrates the strength of the link between the two.

"IT DON'T MEAN A THING IF IT AIN'T GOT THAT SWING"

Duke Ellington is frequently described as "beyond category." His compositions alone show many different influences, including the structural complexity of classical music, the melodic tendencies of African American folk music, the rhythmic vivaciousness of ragtime, and the overall accessibility of mainstream popular song. Yet if you are looking for anything related to Ellington, from biographical information and documentary footage to recordings and scores, you are more likely to find it aligned with jazz than with any other type of music. This might seem like either a simplification or a contradiction—or, even more problematically, a reflection of the role race has played in musical categorization and marketing. Ultimately, though, it stems at least in part from the musical reality in which he lived—a time when jazz was not so much a discrete genre as a method of music making. Jazz has always been—and continues to be—an experimental musical style, one that involves the blending of different sources of inspiration and the introduction of new ideas. Moreover, it emerged at a time when American society was experimenting in much the same way. People of different races, backgrounds, and beliefs were interacting more frequently and more regularly than had previously been the case. New inventions and ideologies were shaping American life—not at the expense of tradition but rather in conjunction with it. The eclectic and innovative nature of Duke Ellington's music is in many ways a mirror of its time—one that embraces the ideology of jazz even though it contains a much broader range of influences.

"It Don't Mean a Thing" is certainly no exception to this. It is recognizable to many listeners, including a fair number who would not identify themselves as fans of jazz—and who might not even be able to identify either the title or the author of the song. It also has a tuneful melody and follows the kind of predictable structure found in other standards. And yet, it is also an excellent example of jazz—full of syncopation and other rhythmic gestures germane to jazz as well as a melodic and harmonic language that draws heavily on blues. More than that, it is an encapsulation of the spirit of the age in which it was written, a song that it often described as prophetic in its title lyric—a prediction of just how vital "swing" rhythm would be in the coming years. Both Terry Teachout and John Edward Hasse use this language in their respective biographies of Ellington, noting that the song's use of the term "swing" predates its prevalence in the American vernacular by three years. The fact that Irving Mills, publisher and longtime professional colleague of Ellington, is formally credited with this title does nothing to diminish Ellington's actual role in developing the concept—and, of course, the song.

Ellington published "It Don't Mean a Thing" in 1931 and recorded it for the first time with singer Ivie Anderson in 1932. The Ellington band issued another celebrated recording of the song in 1943. These two renditions are probably the most familiar, and they are probably the most representative of the song as Ellington crafted it. Many other versions exist, however, all of which remain faithful to the spirit and essence of the song even as they demonstrate its potential for universal appeal and its range of interpretive possibilities. Performances of the song by the legendary French jazzmen Django Reinhardt and Stephane Grappelli, for example, offer an especially good window into just how jazz was able to transport the American Songbook beyond the borders of its own country and its own time.

Jazz had been broadly and widely welcomed into French culture during the First World War. African American soldiers brought ragtime band music to Europe with them, and they were welcomed for both their bravery and their artistry. As a result, a significant number of African Americans—especially entertainers, artists, and writers—immigrated to France after the war. This influx led to a fever for all things related to blues and jazz that lasted throughout the next decade and beyond. By the time Ellington was working and writing, jazz was as much a part of the musical scene in Paris as it was in New York or Chicago. This scene included native Frenchmen inspired by this new American style, men like guitarist Django Reinhardt and violinist Stephane Grappelli.

Without this cultural exchange, the now legendary Reinhardt would obviously have had a very different kind of career. His music would not have been shaped by jazz, to be sure, but he would likely also have missed out on knowing much of the American Songbook. It was largely through musicians like Bix Beiderbecke, Louis Armstrong, and Duke Ellington that Reinhardt and Grappelli encountered this repertoire, which is apparent in their own interpretations. For example, Reinhardt and Grappelli's rendition of "It Don't Mean a Thing" includes large segments of improvisation for both musicians. The rhythms swing in a way that echoes the recordings made by the Ellington band. More importantly, these elements are present even in their renditions of American standards less steeped in jazz tradition than "It Don't Mean a Thing." Their version of "It Had to Be You," for instance, is characterized by fully improvised sections and undulating swing rhythms that run throughout—neither of which can be found in 1920s recordings of the song by popular American artists.

"It Don't Mean a Thing" is also a good example of how the American Songbook continues to cycle through and across the boundaries of not only popular song and jazz but also American theater. It has, for instance, been featured as the opening number of *Swing!*—a 1999 Broadway revue celebrating the era from the mid-1930s to the mid-1940s when swing music dominated American popular culture. Naturally, the Ellington song is a perfect introduction to the show in both musical style and lyrics, especially with its visionary title line. Here, however, the show's creators also emphasize the song's connection to the American Songbook and, by extension, the Broadway musical. Most prominently, the verse is included—a practice that dates back to the days of Jerome Kern and his musicals for the Princess Theater. Also, the vocal style is more heavily shaped by Broadway tradition than by anything else. Ellington's swinging rhythms are still present, of course, but this version of "It Don't Mean a Thing" highlights its structure and tunefulness more than its jazziness. To put it another way, this version shows how a standard can lean toward jazz, popular, or theatrical in a specific interpretation without belonging exclusively to any one of these categories as a song. The fact that this can be seen in a relatively recent rendition of the song shows how standards have collectively maintained this kind of adaptability even as these styles have moved away from one another over the course of time.

Of course, the variety of performances of "It Don't Mean a Thing" over the years has also led to an enormous audience for the song—one that is not confined to place, time, or genre. This demonstrates much of what jazz has accomplished for the American Songbook as a whole: it has fostered an interpretive freedom that took the universality of the standard to new levels and new audiences alike.

"APRIL IN PARIS"

Vernon Duke's biographical profile resembles that of George Gershwin in several ways. Like Gershwin, he was a Russian immigrant with musical talents that allowed him to compose for a variety of arenas, including both the theater (where he wrote under the name Vernon Duke) and the concert hall (where he used his given Russian name, Vladimir Dukelsky). It is difficult to say, of course, but these similar backgrounds and musical gifts may explain why the standards of these two men have been among the most widely interpreted by jazz musicians. Perhaps there is something in the emotional power of their compositions that resonates especially well with the jazz idiom—a spirit distinct from yet remarkably similar to blues.

This is certainly true for "April in Paris," one of Duke's most beloved and familiar songs with lyrics by E. Y. Harburg. To be sure, "April in Paris" has also enjoyed interpretations removed from jazz, including its original use in the 1932 Broadway musical *Walk a Little Faster* as well as the 1952 Doris Day film named for the song. More familiar, however, are the versions by Ella Fitzgerald and Count Basie. These two renditions alone reveal the full range of the song as a jazz standard—and, by extension, the song's emotional and musical richness.

Ella Fitzgerald's rendition is a beautiful expression of longing. This begins with the lyrics, of course, but Fitzgerald communicates their message with sincerity, passion, and exceptional musicality. For instance, she lingers on the repeated notes in each phrase of the melody, as if she is simultaneously resisting and recognizing the need to move forward. This offers listeners a musical illustration of what the lyrics convey—namely, that we can remember the past but we must live in the present. Similarly, she eases gently into the melodic leaps, almost as if she is reluctant to let go of the previous note. This, too, echoes the way in which the song mixes fond recollections of the past with an immediate sense of loss. In short, Fitzgerald's interpretive choices align very closely with the lyrics, which, despite their popular song vocabulary and structure, are remarkably bluesy in their emotional scope. Of course, Duke's melody is constructed in a way that makes this possible, and his rich, lush harmonies lend support to it.

The Count Basie recording, on the other hand, is full of life. It reinterprets the longing sentiments of the lyrics into something more robust—something the protagonist might feel after more time has passed. The memories are still there, but the heartbreak is gone. Now there is an emotional distance that enables the protagonist—who is still there in spirit, even if not in the form of a singer—to move forward with optimism and energy. Nothing makes this more apparent than Basie's exuberant repetition of the song's conclusion—not once but twice.

Interestingly, these two versions are juxtaposed in the 1995 film *Forget Paris* starring Billy Crystal and Debra Winger. The two portray a couple who meet and begin a romantic relationship in Paris only to be separated and reunited numerous times afterward. Not surprisingly, Fitzgerald's rendition is used to accompany a point in the story where the two are living apart from one another. Alternatively, the Basie recording is heard when they are together. This use of different interpretations of the same song—as opposed to two contrasting songs—reminds the audience of what the two characters share even as their moods and desires change.

Such a thing would hardly be possible with anything other than a standard. Its inherent qualities help make even widely different interpretations possible, and its unique relationship to jazz has fostered even more musical diversity. In no other repertoire can listeners find such variety within the recorded history of a particular song.

"BODY AND SOUL"

With music by Johnny Green and lyrics by the team of Edward Heyman, Robert Sour, and Frank Eyton, "Body and Soul" is another example of how the standard and jazz are inextricably linked to one another. In fact, even though it exhibits all the key musical traits of a standard, "Body and Soul" rarely appears alongside the mainstays of the American Songbook—either in lists or in recordings. Instead, it has become the quintessential jazz standard. This is due in large part to influential interpretations of the song by jazz artists in the 1930s and 1940s—interpretations that have overshadowed those made earlier by singers like Gertrude Lawrence and Libby Holman or by bandleaders like Paul Whiteman. Chief among these are the recordings of Coleman Hawkins and Billie Holiday.

Coleman Hawkins's 1939 recording of "Body and Soul" is an iconic piece of jazz history and an excellent example of the way Hawkins improvises. Instead of adding and subtracting notes from the written melody, he creates his own line over the composed harmonies. He moves freely up and down through the notes in the given chords, a technique that has led to the common description of his playing as "vertical" in nature. He does this so fluidly that the resulting music sounds surprisingly melodic—even though repeating his melody would be far more difficult than repeating the original one. Even more impressive is the fact that Hawkins seems to echo Green's melody even though he does not actually play it. In short, he offers a unique interpretation while still honoring the song as it was written.

Notably, Green's evocative harmonic structure facilitates this kind of performance. To be sure, he probably never envisioned such an interpretation. Still, Hawkins would probably not have been inspired to use this approach for a song with a simpler harmonic palette. "Body and Soul," however, takes a number of interesting turns and changes chords rather frequently. It also makes use of less familiar chords as well as those composed of more than the obligatory three notes. This creates more opportunity for melodic experimentation within the composed framework, and Hawkins takes full advantage of it. And, historically speaking, he sets a precedent that has been followed by future generations. Numerous figures in jazz history have used "Body and Soul"—as well as standards with a similar harmonic profile, such as Jerome Kern's "All the Things You Are"—as a rich foundation on which to build their adventurous and ambitious improvisations.

Billie Holiday recorded "Body and Soul" at two different points in her career—once in 1940 and again in 1957. In both cases, she brings a more conventional yet no less creative interpretation of Green's composition. She follows his original melody more closely, but she adds a great deal with respect to articulation and timing—especially in the 1957 version. For instance, she treats the written rhythms in much the same way that Hawkins treats the original melody—something to be sensed rather than overtly heard. She operates within the tempo established by the rhythm section supporting her, yet she sings without any confinement to it. This generates both musical fluidity and a speech-like naturalness in her singing—a rare and beautiful combination, to be sure.

Holiday's approach demonstrates more than her immense prowess as a singer and as a musician, however. It also reveals what happens when jazz and the standard are blended to the fullest extent possible. Her rendition of "Body and Soul" shows the same level of interpretive freedom, improvisational content, and overall innovation as does the one produced years earlier by Coleman Hawkins. Yet her version is also deeply and explicitly communicative on a verbal level, which connects the song to its theatrical roots and to the world of popular song more generally.

JAZZ AND THE PERFORMANCE OF THE AMERICAN SONGBOOK

These examples highlight some of the myriad ways in which jazz and the American Songbook were intertwined in the 1930s and 1940s. There are many others, too, ranging from the relatively predictable—such as the swing-tinged yet easily recognizable version of "Blue Skies" Benny Goodman recorded early in his career—to the more experimental—such as Dizzy Gillespie's use of the chord changes for "I Got Rhythm" as the starting point for his "Salt Peanuts," where the familiar melody is absent. Through all of this exchange, we see how both composition and interpretation were being shaped by people on both sides of the creative coin.

The relationship between jazz and the American Songbook also led to a number of performance conventions that have shaped the recorded history of the standard. Big band instrumentation is perhaps the most obvious of these. Mainstream singers like Frank Sinatra and Tony Bennett spent much of their time in the recording studio along with ensembles dominated by brass and saxophones. This tradition has continued with more recent crooners such as Harry Connick Jr. and Michael Bublé. To be sure, there are plenty of performances with other kinds of instrumental accompaniment, but the prevalence of big bands in recordings of the American Songbook overall shows yet another way in which jazz and the popular standard are difficult to separate. Similarly, improvised solos have remained an important part of the recorded history of the American Songbook. This aspect of performance history comes straight out of the era when jazz had the most influence on the popular standard, and it is one that continues to link the two phenomena.

Yet the most profound results of the exchange between the world of jazz and the American Songbook may well be those that show just how unbounded these two musical spheres have proven to be. Consider, for example, the 1962 collaboration between Duke Ellington and three violinists: Frenchman Stephane Grappelli, a classically trained Dane named Svend Asmussen, and Ellington's longtime friend Ray Nance. Finally released on LP record in 1976, their "Jazz Violin Session" includes the Ellington standards "Take the 'A' Train," "In a Sentimental Mood," and "Don't Get Around Much Anymore." This collection of songs performed by musicians from vastly different backgrounds—and featuring an instrument not especially common in the jazz idiom— reveals the true depth of the relationship between the American Songbook and jazz. Unconventional records like this one offer a remarkable testament not only to how jazz and the American Songbook have interacted but also to how their shared repertoire has brought musicians together and enabled them to experiment.

6

INTERPRETERS OF THE AMERICAN SONGBOOK

Interpreters are an essential part of music making. In the case of the American Songbook, however, they play an especially interesting role— one that is relatively rare in other musical styles and genres. In most forms of classical music, for example, performers typically interpret a wide range of material over the course of their careers. They learn a standard repertoire and share it with their fellow musicians. Some may specialize in a particular period or even a composer, but it is difficult to think of strong associations between a specific piece of classical music and a specific performer. Instead, the music is almost always linked primarily to the composer. Performers simply offer different interpretations, none of which is widely viewed as definitive—more historically accurate or more passionate, perhaps, but not definitive. On the other end of the spectrum, most contemporary popular musicians perform songs written specifically for them—sometimes by others and sometimes by themselves. Their music is almost always linked to their performance of it, to the extent that other renditions are often conceptualized as cover versions, tributes, or reinterpretations rather than simply additional versions. Their music usually belongs to them exclusively in the minds of their listeners.

This creates an interesting dichotomy between these two musical camps. In one case, the composer is the primary voice being heard. In the other, it is the performer who dominates. Interpreters of the American Songbook fit right in the middle of this, possessing traits of both sides. Like classical musicians, they present a repertoire to their listeners—one that is as connected to its creators as to its performers. The music they perform is also shared between them. They do not own it in the way most contemporary popular artists do, either in the popular mindset or in legal terms. Even so, the notion of an original—even if not necessarily definitive—artist does emerge here. We can talk about the first person to sing a particular song, the one who played the biggest role in popularizing it, or the one who sold the most recordings. In this respect, they move toward the realm of contemporary popular music. It is difficult, for instance, to think of Ethel Merman without also thinking of "There's No Business Like Show Business" or to picture Judy Garland without hearing her sing "Over the Rainbow" or "The Man That Got Away." The association is more one-sided here than in contemporary popular culture; the singers are more connected to the songs than the other way around. Still, this phenomenon is present to some extent—and it has everything to do with the evolving nature of musical recording and sound film at the time these songs were being written.

Notably, musicians who occupy this middle-of-the-road role can also be found in jazz, which is true in large part because both jazz and the American Songbook grew up together as musical siblings of the same era—a time when recorded music and films became a major part of American popular culture. When first introduced, these media did three key things. First, they expanded the distribution of specific musical performances. Second, they increased the viable interpretive options for performers. And third, they made listening—as opposed to singing or playing—a more dominant part of popular culture.

Before recordings and films, a song could be widely known but only in written form. This meant that songs were defined almost exclusively by their melodies and lyrics. To be sure, star performers still played a key role in popularizing them by singing them on stage. Publishers clearly recognized this, as they regularly included the names and images of those who introduced songs on the covers of their sheet music. Still, it was the celebrity status of these performers rather than their specific performance of a song that permeated the American consciousness. After all, one singer could only reach so many listeners with personal appearances. It could be a large number in some cases but not a majority of the entire population—nothing like what would be possible with a recorded performance. Moreover, even the most beloved stage performers did not give precisely the same performance more than once. Indeed, the uniqueness of every performance is part of what makes live music making special—something that is still true today. Now, however, recorded music is so much a part of our lives that we can hardly experience a live performance without some kind of preconception of how it should sound—unless, of course, we are entirely unfamiliar with the music. We typically include the most familiar recording of a song in our concept of the song. The sound of the singer's voice, the instruments used, and any number of specific interpretive choices are as important and as defining as the actual notes and rhythms. Such bias was simply not part of the culture that witnessed the rise of the popular standard. It only emerged as the standard developed. As a result, audiences enjoyed performances by different singers and instrumentalists, choosing their favorites without thinking of any one as the original.

For performers, recording technology also opened interpretive doors that had previously remained closed. In particular, it enabled them to engage with their listeners more intimately. Thanks to the introduction of the microphone and the film camera in the 1920s, performers could utilize even the smallest nuances in their faces, bodies, and voices to communicate. In short, they could use techniques that would not have translated in the theater. This brought them closer to their audiences than ever before, at least on an expressive level. And, of course, it led to a much broader range of interpretations for any given song—not to mention a more distinctive version from each person who performed it.

Lastly, the increasing accessibility of recorded music and film made listening to music far more common in American life. Before these technologies, music often required active participation on the part of those who wanted to enjoy it—or at least some of those who wanted to enjoy it. The option of simply listening to music without a performer nearby did not exist. Recording made this possible, however, and it has now become so prevalent that people experience recorded music far more frequently than they do live performances. Of course, it took some time for recorded music to become this ubiquitous. For example, radio—which today features recorded music almost exclusively—aired mostly live performances in the first half of the twentieth century. Similarly, records such as 78s, LPs, and 45s were more limited in where they could be heard than their digital counterparts. They became part of the

American home, but they did not bring music into places like stores or automobiles. Still, recordings had begun to reshape the ways in which Americans were experiencing music by the 1930s, including the American Songbook.

Collectively, these changes gave performers a more central role in how their music was perceived and defined. They had always been essential in both practical and interpretive terms, but their contributions were no longer ephemeral. Instead, their performances became a timeless part of the music, and they became inextricably linked to specific songs. In time, this would even reshape the practice of songwriting, virtually eliminating the notion of a standard from the popular mindset. Initially, however, the changes brought about by the rise of recorded music coexisted with the standard, resulting in a richly varied collection of performances of the repertoire.

Indeed, the recorded history of the American Songbook is a testament to just how many ways these songs can be performed. Their versatility is readily apparent, not only in the sheer number of recordings but also in their musical diversity. Performers have experimented with everything from tempo and dynamics to articulation and vocal style—not to mention arrangements and accompaniment. Notably, though, the essence of each song is always preserved. "I Got Rhythm" is always "I Got Rhythm," whether it is sung by Ella Fitzgerald or Ethel Merman. To put it another way, these are songs that live in performance yet are not defined by any one. They truly are music for the masses—not only a mass of listeners but a mass of interpreters as well.

As such, it would be impossible to discuss every singer who has performed this repertoire. Even a list comprising the most celebrated artists is difficult to compile in any sort of definitive way. For example, well-known singers such as Bing Crosby, Rosemary Clooney, Nat King Cole, Barbra Streisand, and Andy Williams are easily situated in the stylistic vein of the American Songbook, but their coverage of the repertoire over the course of their careers is more limited than a number of other interpreters. They have played a significant role in popularizing certain selections more than the American Songbook as a whole. Conversely, those discussed here have made these songs a major, substantive part of their artistic output. And they represent the range of voice types and stylistic approaches to the repertoire that have been taken over the years.

ETHEL MERMAN

Before she appeared as Mama Rose in *Gypsy* or even Annie Oakley in *Annie Get Your Gun*, Ethel Merman was a force to be reckoned with on Broadway. Her voice was like her stage presence—larger than life and full of brassiness. Her 1930 Broadway debut in *Girl Crazy* made her an overnight success, and it was at this point that George Gershwin insisted that she never work with a voice teacher. Like many others who have heard Merman sing over the years, he liked her voice as it was and did not want to see it change. Any technical improvements such training might have made had the potential to rid Merman of what made her voice so special.

From a historical viewpoint, it is easy to situate Merman among those who originated a style of singing that is commonly known as belting today. This method of vocal production essentially involves a bold, bright, and relatively straight-toned sound—one that typically occurs naturally in the lower and middle registers of the voice but can be extended into the higher register of the voice as well. While not necessarily the best approach for conveying emotional nuance or singing intricate melodic embellishments, belting is very well-suited to powerful, confident musical statements set to straightforward melodic lines. As such, Merman did a wonderful job of introducing standards such as the Gershwins' "I Got Rhythm," Cole Porter's "I Get a Kick Out of You," and Irving Berlin's "There's No Business Like Show Business." Her strong voice and commanding stage presence were all too appropriate for songs like these—songs with potent rhythms, clear melodies, and no hint of sentimentality whatsoever in their lyrics.

Merman would have played an important role in the history of the American Songbook if she had done nothing other than introduce these selections—and others like them—to Broadway audiences. Her particular interpretation of these songs makes her even more noteworthy, however. She exemplifies an interesting and important anomaly in the life of the American Songbook. Her voice is one of the most distinctive ever to be heard on Broadway or on record, and a significant number of the songs she introduced were actually written for her. Yet her renditions have done nothing to diminish the standard qualities of these songs. She has provided us with memorable, inimitable, and truly unique performances of these songs without making them exclusively hers. That is an accomplishment indeed and one that deserves recognition.

In doing this, of course, Merman also demonstrates the versatility of the American Songbook as a whole. This repertoire, even if not in its entirety, can easily accommodate a singer with the unusual talents of Ethel Merman. Of course, Merman represents one end of the interpretive spectrum, one where unique voices are paired with certain songs and song types. The other end, of course, is inhabited by more conventional-sounding voices—though certainly no less extraordinary ones—with the ability to sing across the entire collection. Our next figure, Fred Astaire, belongs to that category.

FRED ASTAIRE

Many people think of Fred Astaire primarily as a dancer and understandably so. For Irving Berlin, however, Astaire was the ideal voice for his songs. As an often-quoted saying goes, Berlin valued Astaire "not because he has a great voice, but because his diction and delivery are so good that he can put over a song like nobody else." To be sure, Astaire communicates lyrics so clearly that he sounds almost as if he is speaking instead of singing—except, of course, that his notes are as lucid and expressive as his words. This gives his interpretations a remarkably natural sound. In this respect, his singing is very much like his dancing. It seems to just happen.

But clarity and effortlessness are only part of what Astaire brings to this repertoire. Because of these qualities, his interpretations draw attention to the songs themselves. He rarely adds much adornment or other personal touches. He simply performs them as written, allowing the music and lyrics to speak for themselves. This is undoubtedly why Irving Berlin favored Astaire as the voice to *introduce* his songs. His performances enable listeners to encounter the song in a relatively unadorned state, bringing audience and songwriter closer together than is often the case.

It is nevertheless true that the warmth of Astaire's voice makes his otherwise straightforward interpretations unusually expressive. His voice may not be dynamic or powerful, but it is pure and sincere. As such, he is able to draw his listeners into a cozy, intimate world where they can feel what he has to say. Of course, it has to be said that Astaire's physicality is also a key component of his interpretations. Because so many of his renditions of these songs have been captured on film, the way he appears shapes the response of his listeners almost as much as the way he sounds. Fortunately, even if not surprisingly, Astaire's body language matches his voice. His classic good looks, his dapper clothes, his fluid footsteps, and his smooth tone all suggest the same sensibility. They all contribute to the elegant feeling that dominates his interpretations.

Nothing gets in the way in Astaire's performances. They are simple in the best sense. He sings with ease and without adding anything superfluous. This quality in Astaire may well explain why people do not tend to associate him as strongly with the songs he has introduced. His performances are as memorable as anyone else's, but their ingenuity lies in how they allow the songs to stand out separately from his own interpretation. It is as though Astaire lets go of the songs as he sings them, enabling them to enjoy a life far beyond his own interpretation. He will always be present in their history, but only in the kind of polite and courteous manner his suave persona would allow.

HELEN FORREST

Helen Forrest is probably the least familiar name discussed here, but her voice may well be recognizable to many who do not know her by name. She sang with three of the biggest names in swing music of the late 1930s and early 1940s: Artie Shaw, Benny Goodman, and Harry James. Under their batons, she sang a wealth of selections from the American Songbook, including "All the Things You Are" with Artie Shaw, "Taking a Chance on Love" and "The Man I Love" with Benny Goodman, and "But Not for Me" and "Skylark" with Harry James.

Obviously, Forrest's interpretations are shaped quite extensively by the other musicians with whom she worked. For one thing, her voice is more central to some of her recordings than others. On some, she only sings one statement of the chorus—or even just a portion of the chorus. On others, she delivers most of the melody as the band accompanies her. Also, she was hardly the one to determine a song's tempo or the overall sound of the band. She had to sing in a manner suited to the stylistic flavor and sound of each ensemble.

Still, even with these limitations, Forrest brings a great deal to her renditions of these songs. Her voice is smooth and flowing, so much so that it almost seems as if she does not need to stop for breath. This gives her performances a wonderful blend of clarity, beauty, and strength. It even makes the times when she sings only briefly seem luxuriously at ease and unhurried. She also has exceptional intonation and pitch accuracy. Even when she chooses to glide between notes for expressive reasons, she always lands precisely where she should. All of this makes her performances very clean—not in any way ordinary but in every way orderly. Perhaps because she was often required to do so and because she then became accustomed to doing so, she sounds much like a featured instrumentalist within the ensemble dynamic—someone who knows how to be expressive as a soloist while still fitting into the sound of the group as a whole. Forrest also used this skill when she recorded duets with Dick Haymes in the later 1940s and 1950s. As demonstrated in their recordings of songs like "It Had to Be You" and "Come Rain or Come Shine," she continued to work as part of a team.

Helen Forrest is an important reminder that these songs were enjoyed far beyond the stage and screen—and that they were performed by a much larger pool of talent than the stars of these arenas. They were an especially important part of the big band repertoire, rendered by both the instrumentalists and the singers who made up these groups. They were also part of a rapidly expanding recording industry, being sung by individuals who at this time lacked the celebrity status of their Broadway and Hollywood counterparts but whose voices were no less familiar—and perhaps even more so. Increasingly, they were the ones heard in homes across the country, bringing these songs to a wide segment of the American public. Helen Forrest was one of these voices, a major contributor to the place of the standard in American life.

BILLIE HOLIDAY

Like Helen Forrest, Billie Holiday was a featured singer with a number of big bands at the height of the swing craze. Of course, in the racially divided culture of the time, Holiday sang with African American bands, including a long stint with the Count Basie Orchestra. The difference, though, is that while Holiday was equally comfortable within an ensemble dynamic, her contributions were both more deeply integrated into the group and more prominently featured. This seems impossible, but Holiday had just the right kind of voice to make it happen.

Holiday is often compared with other instrumentalists as much as with other singers. The reason for this is that her singing gains much of its power from her subtle shifts in tone quality and timbre, something more common in instrumental performance than in vocal performance. She communicates her lyrics as clearly as anyone else, but it is her music that conveys their meaning. To put it another way, she doesn't seem to need lyrics. Instead, she persuades her listeners to pay attention to the way she sings rather than what she sings. This quality makes her sound more like another member of the band—a featured soloist, to be sure, but no more or less featured than a saxophonist whose improvisations precede or follow her. Oddly enough, Helen Forrest was often featured in much the same way, but her singing was more distinct as a vocal solo. In some cases, this made her seem underrepresented rather than equally featured—as though she had not been given enough chance to sing. Holiday, however, almost always stands out, no matter how short or long her actual contribution might be. She accomplishes this by distinguishing herself through means other than her identity as a singer.

For example, Holiday exudes pathos like no one else. She can make almost any line sound utterly forlorn, even when the lyrics and music are not inherently that negative. Carefully nuanced diction and variations in vocal tone give her singing this highly emotional flavor, though listeners are not likely to think about it in this manner. Instead, they are more apt to see her performances as deeply personal, as though the catches in her voice are a reflection of her own losses and heartache. To be sure, Holiday's life had more than its share of sadness and suffering, and this probably had at least some influence on the emotive power of her voice. Even so, we also have to recognize the strength of her interpretive instincts as a musician. She knew what she wanted to convey, and she knew how to do it with her voice.

Holiday also has a wonderful sense of timing. She works within the metric framework without feeling limited by it. She follows the rhythmic patterns written by the composer, but she articulates them as though they are her own ideas. To some extent, this is a reflection of her talent for improvisation. But it is also a broader musical gift that she brings to her listeners—an especially keen awareness that music is a temporal art. As a result, her performances seem neither rushed nor leisurely. They take place in what seems like just the right amount of time, with nothing unnecessary and nothing absent.

In these ways and more, Billie Holiday brings a unique kind of musicality to the American Songbook. She brings to the table a provocative blend of jazz sensibility, vocal flexibility, and instrumental styling. This manner of interpretation is not beloved by everyone, but it is profoundly meaningful for others. And, most importantly, it demonstrates the full breadth of possibilities within the repertoire of popular standards.

JUDY GARLAND

Like many other performers of her era, Judy Garland introduced a number of standards and sang many more. Her place in the history of the American Songbook is special, however, because her work covers such a broad range of its emotional expression and stylistic variety. For example, the optimism of "Over the Rainbow" is a far cry from the bitter heartbreak of "The Man That Got Away." Yet Garland managed to introduce both with remarkable sincerity. One reason for this is the longevity of her career—in particular, the fact that she began working at such an early age. She may not have been a child when she sang "Over the Rainbow," but she was young enough to believably portray one on screen. And that, along with her natural talent, enabled her to convey the song's message in an authentic manner. On the other hand, she introduced "The Man that Got Away" much later, at a point when she appeared not only more mature but also more weathered—the kind of woman who had suffered heartbreak. Of course, Garland had endured many kinds of disappointments in her life by that time, and since much of her audience knew about them, it only heightened her ability to portray such a character on film.

None of this would have mattered, however, if Judy Garland had not had such a strong and versatile voice. Her delivery is powerful at every turn, from her loudest exclamations to her softest utterances. Similarly, her tone ranges from bold and vibrant to subtle and smooth. Indeed, the scope of her vocal prowess has made her an especially influential interpreter of the American Songbook. Garland has done more than sing these songs; she has also set a high bar for anyone else who does so. This is why a number of the songs she has introduced are more strongly associated with her than is often the case for popular standards. In this respect, she is the opposite of someone like Fred Astaire, who allowed songs to move through him as though he were a vessel traveling between songwriter and listener. Garland, on the other hand, seems incapable of such a passive role. She cannot help but leave her distinctive mark on the songs she sings. And yet, even her "signature" songs do not belong exclusively to her. Her interpretations are her own, but the songs still have a life beyond her.

Like Ethel Merman, Judy Garland illustrates the role of unique voices in the history of the American Songbook. Her performances, especially those captured on film, have helped make these songs an enduring part of popular culture. They are memorable and special, with a power all their own. In this way, she demonstrates just how personalized a standard can be. Her renditions show us that the universal qualities of these songs do not in any way limit their ability to be shaped by the voices and personalities who sing them.

ELLA FITZGERALD

No one has done more for the legacy of the American Songbook as a whole than Ella Fitzgerald. She is known as the First Lady of Song for good reason. She is not only one of the most beloved interpreters of the repertoire; she is also the most prolific. Her output includes entire albums dedicated to the individual songbooks of Jerome Kern, Irving Berlin, George and Ira Gershwin, Cole Porter, Harold Arlen, Richard Rodgers and Lorenz Hart, Duke Ellington, and Johnny Mercer. Indeed, by recording them in this manner, she has even helped define the American Songbook like no one else.

Of course, the real value of these recordings is the supreme quality of Fitzgerald's interpretations. Her voice is extremely versatile—so much so that she seems to offer listeners a beautiful blend of everything. The tone of her voice is easy on the ear, matching the smooth quality and precision of singers like Fred Astaire and Helen Forrest. At the same time, she often sounds searing and powerful, with the emotive flavor of performers like Judy Garland and Billie Holiday. This makes her renditions of these songs unusually comprehensive. They fully honor the songs as they are written, but they also explode with personality. Somehow she accomplishes this without any conflict and an amazing sense of naturalness.

Her performances also inhabit a true middle ground between jazz and popular music. Most performers inject some elements of both into their renditions, which is only natural given the mixed heritage and usage of the repertoire. Fitzgerald actually brings them together, in a way that makes her interpretations seem like they do not belong to one style or the other but to both. To put it another way, her recordings demonstrate why the terms "jazz standard" and "popular standard" are essentially synonymous.

As a result, Fitzgerald probably comes closer than anyone else to offering listeners something like a definitive version of the American Songbook. Her performances have a beautiful blend of everything that makes this repertoire, including melodic and lyrical clarity, a strong jazz sensibility, and communicative power. And yet, one of the greatest strengths of her renditions is the way in which she allows the songs to stand on their own. Her singing is like a tribute to the quality of the songs themselves, a statement of admiration on her part. It feels as though she loves the songs—not only as a singer but also as a listener. They are her musical home.

FRANK SINATRA

Frank Sinatra was as much a part of American popular culture in the 1950s as Elvis Presley. Of course, he represented something more traditional in both his repertoire and his demeanor, but he still had a large audience with American youth. Presley was fresh, exciting, and physical, but Sinatra was handsome, suave, and cool. He captivated listeners with his casually smooth sound and the romantic flavor of his songs.

Sinatra sang a wealth of titles from the American Songbook, including "Night and Day" from Cole Porter, "I've Got the World on a String" from Harold Arlen and Ted Koehler, and "Someone to Watch Over

Me" from the Gershwins. In these songs and more, Sinatra sings in a style known as crooning—one that is characterized by a gentle tone, a fair amount of dynamic contrast, and lots of interpretive movement. Even though the timbre of his voice is not all that different from someone like Fred Astaire, his singing lacks that kind of precision and crispness. Instead, he swells from soft to loud, slides from note to note, and breathes whenever it suits him. This makes his interpretations a bit messier and more laid-back—the vocal equivalent of his often-unbuttoned suit jacket and slightly crooked tie. Both the sound and the look suit him, of course; Sinatra doesn't belong in Fred Astaire's perfectly tailored tuxedo, physically or vocally. Instead, he offers listeners a somewhat less-polished version of the American Songbook—one that has proven enormously popular, influential, and historically significant.

One of the reasons for this is the fact that Sinatra was truly a popular recording artist, in the modern sense of the term. His interpretations are audibly indebted to both Broadway and jazz, though few people would associate him with either style very strongly. This was not true for the vast majority of his predecessors. Similarly, he was part of the film industry, but he was not really a film musical star in the manner of Gene Kelly or Fred Astaire—not to mention Judy Garland. Historically speaking, this new interpretive role is especially significant because Sinatra's recording career overlaps with the years when songwriting moved away from the notion of a standard and toward more genre-specific and medium-specific songs. His renditions consequently helped keep the existing repertoire of the American Songbook a part of popular culture. And, of course, they have continued to do so. They also helped shape the next generation of performers—those who would play a different kind of role in keeping these songs alive.

TONY BENNETT

Tony Bennett was born about a decade later than Frank Sinatra, which meant that his early career was more deeply affected by the rising popularity of rock and roll in the 1950s and 1960s than his fellow crooner. Sinatra was already well-established as a recording artist by the time this new style emerged, making it relatively easy for him to retain his audience. Bennett, however, had just come onto the scene in the early

1950s, so his initial hits were followed by a less-stable period in terms of recording contracts, sales, and overall reception. Bennett never really disappeared from the public eye and ear, though, especially when he recorded standards written in his own time like "The Best Is Yet to Come."

Generally speaking, Bennett's singing style is very similar to that of Sinatra. He brings the same casual approach to his music, and his interpretations have a similar character as a result. They are still distinctive, however, especially with respect to vocal timbre and improvisational liberty. Compared to Sinatra's smooth sound, Bennett's voice has a slightly raspy quality to it. It is certainly not harsh, but it is not clean or polished either. This trait has only grown as Bennett has aged, making his more recent work even rougher around the edges. As with Billie Holiday, however, a seemingly less-than-ideal sound has proven to be something many listeners admire and enjoy—something that gives meaning to his interpretations. To put it another way, fans of Bennett would hardly have him sound any other way, and many would probably not listen to him if he did.

Bennett also typically takes more liberties than does Sinatra—not to mention most other interpreters of the American Songbook. For example, he sometimes speaks selected lyrics for contrast, he often embellishes the melodic line, and he frequently plays around with rhythm and tempo. To be sure, most singers do this to some extent, but Bennett's recordings incorporate more than most. As a result, even his tribute albums like *Perfectly Frank* (featuring songs popularized by Sinatra) and *Steppin' Out* (featuring songs popularized by Fred Astaire) offer listeners something that sounds familiar and new at the same time.

In recent years, Bennett has further expanded his sphere of influence and the audience for the American Songbook by collaborating with a number of contemporary recording artists. Performers as diverse as Lady Gaga and Paul McCartney have joined him in singing popular standards, and the results have proven tremendously popular. In these duets and in his solo work, Bennett has made a reasonably successful attempt to return these songs to their original status as popular music for the masses—songs that everyone knows.

HARRY CONNICK JR.

Harry Connick Jr. has had an unusually varied career in the music and film industries. His musical influences range from jazz to funk and pop. He writes many of his own songs but is equally well-known for his renditions of familiar favorites. He has taken on non-singing roles in film, and he has contributed music to films in which he does not act. As a result of this eclecticism, the American Songbook is only a relatively small part of Connick's creative output. Yet this part of his output is probably the one for which he is best known, and his performance of the repertoire has proven enormously significant.

Harry Connick Jr. made his first major contribution to the American Songbook when he and his jazz trio provided much of the soundtrack for *When Harry Met Sally*. Despite its then contemporary setting in the 1980s, the film was filled with songs of the past—a number of popular standards as well as a few traditional songs, show tunes, and classical melodies. Some of the standards were sung by voices like Ella Fitzgerald and Frank Sinatra, evidence that their recorded versions of these songs could still resonate with audiences years—even decades—after they were first performed. Others, though, were rendered by Connick and his instrumental collaborators, offering listeners a fresh voice to go along with the familiar melodies. His performances proved overwhelmingly popular, and this success led him to other projects dominated by standards—including another romantic comedy soundtrack for *Sleepless in Seattle* (1993) as well as the albums *Songs I Heard* (2001) and *Your Songs* (2009).

One reason for his widespread appeal is that, like Ella Fitzgerald, Connick performs with an unusually balanced mixture of popular and jazz elements. This enables him to resonate with fans in both camps—not only as a singer but as a pianist. In some ways, the fact that many of his performances have been marketed alongside Hollywood films has made it easier for him to honor the mixed heritage of these songs and the more fluid genre landscape in which they arose. After all, the broad distribution of the film automatically situated its soundtrack in the realm of popular music, enabling Connick and his collaborators to inject as much jazz as they liked without worrying about how it might affect the labeling or marketing. Even so, Connick's own ingenuity in bringing the two sides of this repertoire together should not be dismissed. He is a strong improviser with clear jazz sensibilities, but he is also a smooth-toned singer with a crooner-like sound. This combination is remarkably well-suited to the American Songbook as a repertoire—which probably explains why it has played such an important part in Connick's uniquely varied career.

DIANA KRALL

Diana Krall introduced herself with the American Songbook in the 1990s. Her debut album, *Stepping Out*, featured a long list of favorites from the repertoire including "This Can't Be Love," "On the Sunny Side of the Street," "42nd Street," and the quintessential jazz anthem "Body and Soul." Standards have continued to be a major part of her output ever since, and she brings a truly unique sensibility to these songs. Her use of a small, intimate ensemble makes her recordings sound very different from those of the big band singers, but there is more to her unusual sound than a smaller dynamic range and more limited instrumental timbres. There is also something special about the way her voice integrates into the group that distinguishes her performances.

Like Billie Holiday, Diana Krall has an instrumentalist's sense of timing and ensemble awareness—as one might expect from someone who is also a pianist. Yet Krall uses this skill in a different way than does Holiday. She plays a great deal with texture and balance in her recordings, almost pushing her vocal contributions into the background at times. She never disappears, of course, but her voice does not have the same performative presence as most singers. She invites you to come into the music rather than offering it to you, and the unusually low register of her voice makes this especially effective.

This gives the songs she sings a very intimate and even meditative flavor—a stark contrast to how many of them were originally rendered in far more robust and presentational ways. Yet her renditions are as interesting and as communicative as any ever made. They are provocative in their subtlety, if such a thing is possible. And, of course, they show just how malleable the American Songbook can be. These songs were not written for the kind of interpretive approach Diana Krall uses, but they sound remarkably well-suited to it regardless. Krall would hardly have been drawn to them otherwise. Her performances of the American Songbook are thus an important part of its interpretive history—if for no other reason than their distinctiveness.

MICHAEL BUBLÉ

Frequently dubbed a neo-crooner, Michael Bublé sings in the manner of Frank Sinatra and Tony Bennett. His voice is smooth and fluid, his diction is clear, and his musicality is relaxed. Notably, he also projects much the same image of casual coolness as these time-honored predecessors, often appearing in a clean-cut suit with a loosened—or absent—tie. And, of course, his repertoire is dominated by the American Songbook—not only in actual songs but in style and substance as well. For example, his cover versions of more recent popular hits are arranged to sound like they could have been written much earlier—with a swing band orchestra as accompaniment and a more jazz-oriented sensibility for rhythm and phrasing. Even his newly composed songs are more stylistically indebted to the popular standard than to any other song type—undoubtedly because he, as songwriter, is so heavily influenced by and devoted to these selections.

Despite his obvious dedication to the musical traditions that formed and disseminated the American Songbook in its heyday, however, Bublé is not stuck in the past. His interpretations are both fresh and original—perhaps not in their overall soundscape but in their interpretive details. For one thing, Bublé sings with exceptional clarity of tone. His voice has the same kind of purity found in Fred Astaire but with far more power and flexibility. As a result, he communicates impressively well and with great dynamic range. For another, he emulates the style of earlier musical arrangements without duplicating them. His orchestra is a big band in its instrumentation, yet it does not sound like the bands of Benny Goodman, Artie Shaw, or Nelson Riddle—all of whom accompanied singers of the American Songbook in earlier generations. Instead, his musicians blend together bits of theatrical style, jazz, and contemporary musical flavor to generate something that sounds both traditional and modern at the same time.

As a result, Michael Bublé has done more than introduce these songs to a new generation; he has actually made them part of that new generation. This is tremendously significant because it does more than honor the past. It makes these songs current.

INTERPRETATION AND OWNERSHIP

Even with all of their differences, these singers do share some interesting traits that have inclined them toward the American Songbook as a repertoire. Their voices, for instance, all sound relatively natural. They use microphones, but they do not depend on this or any other technology as an actual interpretive tool. Instead, they rely on the inherent resonance of their voices and their technical ability as musicians. Similarly, they are all rooted either in the theater or in jazz as a stylistic starting point for their interpretations. This is undoubtedly responsible at least in part for drawing them to the American Songbook in the first place, and it results in a collection of recordings with a similar musical palette—one that uses the same sonic colors, albeit in a wide variety of ways.

These commonalities give them what might be called a collective ownership of the American Songbook. Instead of belonging to one particular singer, these standards belong to a community of singers—these and many others like them—who share this general kind of vocal production and stylistic foundation. This still allows for a wide range of interpretive choices and methods, allowing each performer to bring something special to each song. Yet it also creates a sense of shared history and camaraderie among the singers of this repertoire. They do not operate as competitors within the music marketplace but rather as fellow advocates and devotees of the songs they love. Those who are younger honor those who have come before them, whether by working collaboratively with them or by simply acknowledging that their own performances are indebted to their work.

This communal sense of ownership also extends to the composers and lyricists of these songs. Performers of this repertoire are almost always eager to praise the men and women who crafted the music and words they present. Consider, for example, Ella Fitzgerald's series of albums dedicated to the work of specific songwriters. Such an effort speaks volumes about the admiration Fitzgerald and her fellow collaborators have for the music they present to their listeners. She honors them simply by singing their songs as an important collection of American music. And, of course, the songwriters have made their contribution to this community of ownership by simply allowing others to perform their work. This might seem like a small thing, especially since most of the authors of the American Songbook did not make performing a major part of their career. Still, even those who did—such as Johnny Mercer and Duke Ellington—also made their work accessible for others to interpret, which was a necessary first step in creating this kind of creative ownership.

This willingness to share music is virtually nonexistent in today's popular music. Songwriters who also perform rarely release their material to other artists. And, if they do, they often still hold on tightly to their possession in some way—whether legal, cultural, or artistic. Similarly, performers who rely on other creative talents for their songs typically acknowledge the men and women behind their success in relatively obscure ways—which means they are not nearly as well-known as the artists who make their songs familiar to the American public. In short, personal ownership has largely overtaken communal ownership in the realm of popular music over the past few decades.

This shift resulted from numerous changes within the music industry beginning in the 1950s—changes that fragmented the industry and reshaped the ways Americans conceptualized a song. It therefore speaks volumes about the American Songbook and the artists who have continued to interpret it that it has continued to nurture this communal sense of ownership even in an atmosphere where it is not the norm. It shows that these songs are a cultural force to be reckoned with—one that would be affected by these changes without disappearing from the American musical landscape.

7

THE AMERICAN SONGBOOK IN THE 1950S AND 1960S

After years of expanding its audience, influence, dramatic utility, and interpretive range, the American Songbook faced a new world by the 1950s. One change, and probably the most obvious one, was the emergence of rock and roll. This new blues-based music was the cultural equivalent of swing twenty years earlier, offering listeners a fresh kind of dance music filled with energy. The entertainment industry responded much differently to rock and roll than it had to swing, however, and it is this response—more than the new musical style itself—that affected the American Songbook.

Most importantly, this response was not coming from a cohesive entertainment industry. Broadway, Hollywood, and the increasingly dominant recording industry had gradually become essentially independent units, operating with their own respective goals and audiences. As a result, most songwriters were now devoting their efforts to one of these arenas rather than hoping to write something that could be popularized through all three. Marketing practices were also being shaped by this division, which was gradually eliminating the kind of mass audience for which the American Songbook had been written. Instead, songs were largely being marketed to a single demographic—such as, in the case of rock and roll, the middle-class American teenager.

To look at it through another lens, the converging forces that had helped foster the development of the American Songbook were shifting away from one another and developing different priorities. Broadway was becoming increasingly insular, a place where most songwriters devoted their energy to the musical and dramatic structure of their shows rather than the reception of their songs more broadly. As this happened, Hollywood began taking fewer cues from New York. To be sure, some of the most successful stage shows of the 1950s and 1960s were still adapted into film musicals, especially those written by established, recognizable songwriters capable of drawing in audiences. In general, however, musical films were becoming a smaller component of the film industry and the influence of Broadway on Hollywood was diminishing.

Instead, Hollywood was becoming increasingly tied to the recording industry—a pairing that was probably inevitable. After all, these two branches of the entertainment business were both based in California by this time, and they were both recorded media. This means that they both inherently emphasized the role of the performer in the life of a song—far more than a composer, a lyricist, or an arranger. As such, films remained a viable marketplace for established standards, but they rarely fostered the development of new ones. Alternatively, songs were either integrated into films in a recorded version already popular with audiences or they were written for a film with a particular performer in mind—whether it was someone starring in the film or someone who would sing it as part of the soundtrack.

Jazz continued to enrich and develop the established repertoire of popular standards in many ways, but most musicians in this arena were also moving away from the mainstream in one of two ways. Some rendered standards in such a traditional fashion that they did not sound fresh enough to gain new listeners. Others experimented with their potential to such an extent that they became largely unrecognizable as anything other than avant-garde. This increasingly divided world of jazz therefore remained a place where the standard would be both preserved and advanced, but not a place where new songs of this type would be developed.

These kinds of changes, which accompanied the rise of rock and roll in the 1950s and 1960s, did several things to the American Songbook. First, they pushed these songs out of the limelight. Standards remained a part of popular culture, but they were now one component of a broader musical spectrum. Second, these changes signaled a drastic decline in the creation of new standards. The demand for songs on universal themes suitable for use in all kinds of media simply was not there anymore. Third, they started to reshape the way listeners think about songs. Instead of a melodic template ready to be sung, the popular song was fast becoming a single recorded performance—one that could be repeated but not reinterpreted.

WHAT HAPPENED TO THE SONG

By the 1950s, technological innovations and new business tactics were giving the recorded song unprecedented importance within the music industry as a whole. People were increasingly buying music in recorded form, which had enormous implications beyond diminishing sales of sheet music. For one thing, it meant that fewer and fewer Americans were participating in the world of popular music. A small number would still create their own renditions of a song, and some would sing along with recordings, but there was no need for the general public to reproduce songs entirely on their own. They could truly be nothing more than listeners if they chose—and a majority did just that. As a result, recordings became increasingly definitive. Repetition of a single recorded performance began to cement that specific rendition in the mind of the listener so strongly that it gradually displaced melody and lyrics as the very identity of the song.

This obviously changed the approach of record production substantially. Now, the goal was not simply to capitalize on the latest song hit by recording a popular version but to actually produce a hit. That led many producers to focus on developing star recording artists who could develop a following. In short, the emphasis became the performer rather than the song. Both were still needed, of course, but the former replaced the latter as the primary focus of the industry, especially from a marketing standpoint.

The quintessential example of this phenomenon is the star recording artist most synonymous with the music business in the 1950s—Elvis Presley. Nurtured by producer Sam Phillips, Presley became a celebrity primarily with songs written by and for other singers—including a number of African American artists. He made them hits, of course, but he did so at the expense of the other talents involved in creating and introducing them. And, in the long run, it became difficult for anyone else to render them without being considered an imitator.

This was hardly an environment conducive to the production of popular standards. The style and structure of the standard were inherently
not a problem, but there was a decreasing need within the industry to
create music with broad applicability. In fact, songs written for a specific purpose became far more marketable in this emerging situation. Notably, it did not diminish the appeal of existing standards; their familiarity enabled them to retain their commercial value and continue to be
recorded. But this shift did not encourage the creation of new songs
with these same traits.

WHAT HAPPENED ON BROADWAY

Broadway gave birth to the standard, and it was also the first to witness
its departure from the pinnacle of popular culture. By the 1950s,
Broadway itself had begun to drift away from its central place in
American musical life. To some extent, this was the result of outside
forces; the rising popularity of films, music recordings, radio, and eventually television would have made it impossible for the theater to retain
the kind of grip it had once held on the American public. Still, changes
within the Broadway community also contributed to this shift. First and
foremost, Broadway was making increasingly lofty goals for itself. With
the same patriotism and inventiveness that had led to the development
of musical comedy in the 1920s, producers and directors continued to
aim for distinctly American works that could rival their European
counterparts in both musical quality and dramatic power. Especially by
mid-century, they wanted to show that music on stage could be something more than entertainment. It could be poignant, real, and ultimately human. In short, it could be art.

Now, it is not hard to make a case that at least some selections in the
American Songbook are in fact works of art. Similarly, it is entirely
appropriate to recognize the men and women who wrote them as artists—even exceptionally gifted ones. Still, the original purpose of these
songs was not to be art—at least in the modernist and postmodernist
use of the term. Instead, they were designed to be entertaining and
popular. The majority of the songwriters behind the American Songbook wanted their work to be good, but they also wanted it to sell. Most
of them viewed music as an opportunity for a better life for themselves

and their families; many of them had grown up in poor immigrant families with few options for earning anything more than a meager living. Songwriting, however, was a lucrative business, and for those with the talent and drive to pursue it, it had the potential to reap great rewards.

By mid-century, however, this mindset was no longer dominant on Broadway. Artistic goals had risen to the fore, especially with respect to the plots of musical shows and the way in which music was used within them. Plots were becoming more serious overall; many were still love stories and had their humorous moments, but purely farcical plots were largely disappearing from the Broadway landscape. Not surprisingly, this shift was complemented by songs that were increasingly tied to specific characters and dramatic circumstances.

The kind of stories and songs seen in *Show Boat* in 1927 had become a staple by the mid-1940s, in large part because Oscar Hammerstein II continued producing works in this vein with his new professional partner, Richard Rodgers. This began in 1943 with *Oklahoma!*, a production involving more true-to-life characters, a richer and more complicated love story, and songs that are so much a part of the plot that they seem to come right out of it rather than fit into it. "Oh, What a Beautiful Morning," for instance, opens the show in an amazingly natural way. Curly sings it as though no one were listening, without any attempt to be presentational at all. This kind of "ordinary" or "everyday" singing continues throughout most of the production. Even the now-familiar anthem "Oklahoma" occurs as part of the town social, where music and dancing are to be expected—and not as in earlier backstage musicals, where the characters "perform" their songs. Here, it is a community of people who make music for their own enjoyment rather than for the purpose of entertaining others. In short, Rodgers and Hammerstein eliminated the need to use the entertainment industry as a backdrop by finding other kinds of characters who sing and dance in their everyday lives—not in a professional capacity but simply as part of their daily experience. This fosters the development of real characters and powerful songs uniquely suited to them. It does not, however, lead to an abundance of songs with the characteristics of the standard. "Oh, What a Beautiful Morning" is universal in its expression, for instance, but "Surrey with the Fringe on Top"—which follows on the heels of the opening song—is far more specific to its dramatic setting. Notably,

"Surrey with the Fringe on Top" is probably as familiar today as any other song from the show, but this is because *Oklahoma!* has proven so enduringly popular as a piece of theater—not because the song has enjoyed a significant life outside the show. In this respect, it exemplifies how the shows of Rodgers and Hammerstein set the stage musical on a path that would ultimately generate fewer and fewer standards. Their work remained rooted in the world that produced the American Songbook, but it also began to grow in a new direction.

This new direction was taken further by the next generation of Broadway songwriters, including people like John Kander and Fred Ebb, Cy Coleman, and Stephen Sondheim. If they happened to have a popular hit, so be it, but their aim was to create a cohesive musical show. And, to their credit, they created not only some of the most successful but also some of the most influential productions ever staged on Broadway. For Broadway fans, the songs from shows like *Cabaret* (Kander and Ebb, 1966), *Sweet Charity* (Coleman and Dorothy Fields, 1966), and *A Little Night Music* (Sondheim, 1973) are as familiar and as memorable as any in the American Songbook. Yet only two of these— "Cabaret" and "Send in the Clowns"—have enjoyed even moderate popularity outside their original context. And it is not because these songwriters departed stylistically from their Broadway predecessors in some drastic way. Sondheim is more harmonically adventurous than most, and his melodies often lack the catchiness of a Gershwin tune. Yet even his songs are ultimately no more challenging to the ear than Jerome Kern's "All the Things You Are" or Cole Porter's "Night and Day." In short, their more limited appeal lies not in their musical complexity alone but rather in how they have been shaped by and according to their dramatic purpose. Their lyrics are more like dialogue and soliloquy, which situates them beautifully on stage. Similarly, their music is part of a continuum that runs through the show, with introductory utterances, recurring themes, and so forth. In this respect, they are more like operatic arias—extractable as discrete selections but ultimately part of a larger musical framework.

This shift toward score writing has continued to shape Broadway in more recent years, especially in the form of epic musicals like *Les Misérables* (1987) and *Ragtime* (1996). There have been other interesting influences as well, however. Most notably, popular culture has revisited Broadway. Popular films have been made into stage musicals, songs popularized through the recording industry have been compiled to form various kinds of shows, and the style of contemporary rock and popular music has permeated the Broadway realm in numerous ways—from the introduction of the electric guitar and other amplified instruments in orchestra pits to the adoption of rock-style vocals on stage. Interestingly, though, this more recent reconnection with the entertainment industry is largely one-sided. Broadway is borrowing regularly from films and recordings, but the reverse is happening far less frequently. In short, Broadway's new relationship with popular culture is very different from the one it had in the early twentieth century. Then, it was the incubator and exporter of popular culture. Now, it is functioning more like Hollywood in the 1930s and 1940s—replicating ideas from another form of entertainment.

As a result, Broadway songwriters since the 1950s have not been the men and women behind the popular music landscape. Some have written innovative and influential musical scores, but few of these have infiltrated American popular culture more broadly. Others have reinterpreted mainstream musical styles, but few have captured the kind of audience that Broadway once enjoyed. This is not inherently a bad thing, of course, but recognizing these changes helps us understand how and why Broadway has not been generating popular standards like it once did.

One thing Broadway has maintained from the age when it produced the American Songbook is an environment where songs are performed by a range of singers rather than a single star. New songs and scores may be written with particular voices in mind, but the long-term success of any Broadway show depends not only on its original cast but also on the men and women who eventually replace them in their roles. In short, composers and lyricists working on Broadway are still writing with this kind of versatility in mind—something that is no longer true for the entertainment industry more broadly.

WHAT HAPPENED IN HOLLYWOOD

Because Hollywood followed Broadway in its use of popular standards, these songs continued to play a pivotal role in films after their importance was declining on stage. In fact, MGM drew special attention to the American Songbook as a repertoire in the 1950s with films like *An American in Paris* (1951), *Singin' in the Rain* (1952), and *The Band Wagon* (1953), each of which was created around the catalog of a particular songwriting team—George and Ira Gershwin, Arthur Freed and Nacio Herb Brown, and Howard Dietz and Arthur Schwartz, respectively. With Arthur Freed at the helm, MGM also produced other successful musicals in this traditional vein, including *Gigi* (1958) and *My Fair Lady* (1964). Twentieth Century Fox followed suit with adaptations of successful Broadway musicals throughout the 1950s and early 1960s, most notably those of Richard Rodgers and Oscar Hammerstein. In short, the film musical was doing its utmost to keep the musical style of the popular standard in the ears of the American public even as rock and roll emerged on the scene.

Still, change was coming; it just happened a bit later. Songwriting teams like Rodgers and Hammerstein and Alan Lerner and Frederick Loewe—who crafted the score of *My Fair Lady*—were among the last to build a career on both coasts. And, as Broadway composers moved toward a more specialized kind of dramatic musical work, songwriters in California were driven in one of two directions: (1) writing individual popular songs designed primarily for the recording studio and possibly a specific scene in a film, or (2) writing the kind of full-length film scores used before the advent of sound film—ones designed to take audiences through the emotional landscape of the story. Those in the latter category obviously had little interest in popular song; their job was to accompany and enhance the drama. More importantly, those in the former category were largely writing without any dramatic context in mind, so their work was shaped by the recording industry more than anything else—an industry that, as noted above, had changed drastically since the early standards were being written.

As a result, Hollywood was gradually losing its place of prominence in the dissemination of popular song—except in the realm of animation. From the pioneering efforts of Walt Disney to more recent productions from studios such as Pixar and DreamWorks, the animated film has introduced a plethora of new songs to audiences—far more than any other film genre in recent decades. Notably, some of these films have adopted a contemporary Broadway style—and have consequently featured stage performers on their soundtracks. The Disney hit *Frozen* (2013) is a good example of this approach, and its songs have become enormously popular through the success of the film. Still, the songs are indelibly linked to the film and have not been widely marketed on recordings other than the film soundtrack. As was the case for *Oklahoma!* decades earlier, it is the appeal of the production as a whole—as opposed to the use of the songs outside the original context—that has made the songs familiar to a large portion of the American public. On the other side of the coin are films like *Despicable Me 2* (2013), which was responsible for introducing the Pharrell Williams song "Happy." In this case, the song was also marketed individually beyond the context of the film. It was widely heard on the radio, appeared on Williams's studio album *Girl* (2014), and was produced as a music video. Still, even this range of marketing techniques is far less comprehensive than what happened in the age of the American Songbook. The song has not been part of any stage show, and more importantly, it has not been presented in different versions created by multiple performers. Instead, it is a product of the recording industry—and an example of how that industry has changed since the 1950s. Before that time, there simply was no such thing as a definitive recording of any one song. Now it is difficult to imagine anything other than a single recording as the identity of a popular song.

WHAT HAPPENED IN JAZZ

Throughout the ages dominated by ragtime, early jazz, and swing, popular music had been shaped so deeply by these musical forces that there was little if any call to think of them as distinct from one another. On the negative side, this reality often diluted the latest jazz music to emerge and, more problematically, overshadowed the musicians responsible for the innovation—many of whom were already marginalized in American society because of their race. Even so, it also fostered the view that a song could be the foundation for almost any kind of interpretation. It created an atmosphere in which popular songs could serve as templates for a wide range of performers.

It was this atmosphere that had facilitated such an intimate relationship between popular song and jazz, and its disappearance consequently led to their separation. As swing faded from popularity in the late 1940s and 1950s, jazz moved in new directions that did not have the same widespread appeal as earlier styles. In fact, many jazz musicians strove to make a conscious move away from the mainstream. Bebop, for example, was not conducive to dancing—something that had been synonymous with all earlier styles of jazz. Instead, it was designed as a listening music—and one that challenged listeners to go beyond their comfort zone. It featured more dissonant sounds, extreme tempos, and less-audible melodies than anything that preceded it. Even cool jazz, which emerged on the scene shortly after bebop, did not develop the kind of mainstream following swing had enjoyed. Although it was more musically conservative than bebop, it was fueled by an aloof attitude that simply did not seek or attract a broad audience.

Needless to say, these styles also had little influence on more widely popular ones. They became alternatives to the rock and roll market, and there was virtually no connection between the two—musically or culturally. For example, there was nothing in jazz to parallel the kind of stardom seen in the popular music market. There were celebrated musicians, of course, but they were not celebrities like rock and pop stars. Similarly, jazz thrived on its underground status. Its listeners reveled in the fact that this music was not heavily commercialized. In this respect, jazz followed a path somewhat similar to Broadway. It was driven by artistic goals rather than a desire to reach the masses.

Oddly enough, the American Songbook often served as a foundation for this artistic exploration. For example, Dizzy Gillespie's "Salt Peanuts"—an iconic example of early bebop—uses the harmonic and rhythmic underpinnings of Gershwin's "I Got Rhythm." This kind of borrowing shows the extent to which this repertoire had permeated jazz and the interpretive freedom jazz artists felt in using it by the middle of the century—a freedom made by the structure of the songs themselves. In fact, there are many other famous examples of this kind of thing from a wide variety of jazz artists—John Coltrane's reinterpretation of the Rodgers and Hammerstein classic "My Favorite Things," Miles Davis's rendition of the Rodgers and Hart song "My Funny Valentine," and, more recently, Anthony Braxton's highly dissonant version of the Gershwin tune "Embraceable You" are just a few of these.

The American Songbook has thus been both preserved and reinvented in the hands of jazz musicians. But jazz has not provided an environment that fostered the development of new standards in more recent years. And, because it has moved away from the mainstream itself, it has not widened the audience for the repertoire as it once did.

WHAT HAPPENED TO THE AUDIENCE

A quick glance at the timeline at the beginning of this book shows that listeners were obviously still enjoying the American Songbook in the 1950s and 1960s. Ella Fitzgerald and Frank Sinatra alone generated enough albums during this period to attest to the enduring appeal of the repertoire. But this only points to the fact that standards were in fact becoming a repertoire at this time. Generally speaking, they were no longer in development—for all of the reasons already discussed. Instead, they were being collected and archived as an important historical achievement—one that was still very popular but not new. Their audience was still substantial, but it was nothing like what it had once been.

Tony Bennett's career shows this with remarkable clarity. As a younger peer of Frank Sinatra, he began singing standards with great success in the 1950s and early 1960s. By the late 1960s, however, he struggled to find the same kind of mass audience that he had enjoyed in the previous decade. He suffered from the growing sense among record producers that these songs—and even newly composed ones in a similar style—could not compete with rock and roll in the recorded music market. As Bennett writes in his autobiography, "The record companies thought that rock and roll was all anybody would ever want to hear from that point on . . . [and] they gradually lost interest in anything else." His kind of music, what is now often identified as traditional pop, was increasingly being shunned as old-fashioned by the recorded music market—and neither Bennett nor anyone else could change that. The powers that be had decided that the audience for this music was shrinking, and so it did.

It is all too poignant, then, that Bennett has played a leading role in redefining the American Songbook in the twenty-first century as something more than historical. His albums of the past ten years have made it clear that these songs remain not only culturally relevant but also commercially viable. Of course, he has not done this alone; he has purposely collaborated with highly visible performers in contemporary pop music such as Amy Winehouse and Lady Gaga to draw in the latest generation of listeners. This approach is more than a marketing tactic, however. It has also recognized and renewed the innate nature of these songs as music for everyone—performers as well as listeners. As a result, Bennett and his fellow devotees have reinstated the American Songbook within the musical mainstream in a way that has the potential to truly capitalize on the timeless nature of its contents. Thanks to him and numerous other champions, this repertoire is being heard almost as frequently and as widely as it was in the early twentieth century.

8

THE AMERICAN SONGBOOK TODAY

The American Songbook is alive and well today. It continues to be heard in each of the arenas that came together to give it life—the Broadway stage, the Hollywood film, and the world of jazz. But it has also come back into the wider American consciousness in a way that, while not equal to its initial mass popularity, comes closer than anything it has experienced since that time. Even if the repertoire is not comprehensively being heard by a large audience, numerous individual songs are enjoying a much wider group of listeners, both young and old.

In an indirect way, the renewed correspondence between different media within the entertainment industry has helped set the stage for this to happen. For example, there has been a remarkable resurgence in musical films since the beginning of the twenty-first century—and not just in the world of animation. While few of these new productions have actually included popular standards in their soundtracks, their increasing presence in popular culture has nevertheless reopened many eyes and ears to the musical style of Broadway that gave birth to the American Songbook and pointed out that songs can both belong to and transcend a specific dramatic setting. Similarly, the emergence of jazz artists interested in crossing over into the mainstream and the interest in jazz among mainstream artists have renewed the notion that pop music and jazz can in fact coexist and borrow from one another. Moreover, some Broadway artists have ventured into mainstream popular culture via the recording studio—not only on soundtracks but also on song collection albums. In short, an industry that had been putting up barriers is now seeing more and more of them breaking apart in some ways—not disappearing, exactly, but not being entirely preserved either.

In this spirit, the notion of what constitutes a popular standard is coming into question. Even though the repertoire is not growing as it once did, recording artists are suggesting that it might be expanded by association to include songs that share some aspects of the standard. Some contemporary songs written for Broadway, for example, exhibit certain stylistic traits of the standard. "Come Down from the Tree" by Stephen Flaherty and Lynn Ahrens, and "The Stars and the Moon" by Jason Robert Brown are among the many examples of this. Each possesses a tuneful, catchy melody; a timeless message; and a balanced blend of repetition and contrast. And Broadway stars are bringing these songs together with those of the American Songbook in recording and performance.

Similarly, some classic pop songs of the late twentieth century have the same kind of tunefulness and broad applicability as the standard even though they have retained a strong association with their original artist. These include songs like Paul McCartney's "Yesterday," Billy Joel's "Just the Way You Are," Elton John's "Your Song," and Sting's "Fields of Gold." In some cases, contemporary artists are even reinterpreting them in ways that highlight their standard qualities, often alongside selections from the American Songbook.

All of this is breathing new life into the American Songbook. It will always retain its historical place, but time is demonstrating that it is more than just music of the past. Instead, it continues to be music with broad applicability and enduring appeal—a collection of songs that is thriving even in an industry far different than the one that gave it birth. Many performers are part of this, and they come from the full range of musical spheres that have long nurtured this repertoire: Broadway, jazz, Hollywood, and popular music.

AUDRA MCDONALD AND BRIAN STOKES MITCHELL

In 1996, Audra McDonald and Brian Stokes Mitchell appeared together in a musical version of the E. L. Doctorow novel *Ragtime*. The story takes place in the years just before the American Songbook was written—right after the turn of the twentieth century—and it features a number of actual historical characters as well as fictional ones. Many of its songs, written by Stephen Flaherty and Lynn Ahrens, hearken back to this period as well. Some attempt to recapture the vibrant rhythmic flavor of ragtime dance music and vaudeville novelty songs; others emulate the style of love songs and narrative ballads popular at the time. Some are more audibly indebted to earlier music than others, but one thing they all share is the need to be sung by singers with a traditional, or perhaps even old-fashioned, Broadway sensibility. As such, *Ragtime* differed in its musical style from most other new shows being staged in the 1990s, many of which were adaptations of films filled with contemporary pop culture references and songs written by and for rock and pop rock voice types. Instead, it had more in common with the revivals of that period, shows that revisited and revived earlier Broadway successes more closely linked to the American Songbook in both musical style and dramatic substance.

As such, it is hardly surprising that McDonald and Mitchell were chosen for their respective roles in the production. They are skilled actors, to be sure, but it is their voices for which they are each best known. McDonald's blend of classical training and earthy power create a sound that is strikingly beautiful, and her interpretive ability is equally impressive. Mitchell's warm and robust baritone demands an audience's attention, and it is as potent when he sings quietly as when he resonates throughout an auditorium. These qualities are much the same as those of the stars who first introduced the American Songbook on Broadway in the musicals of Jerome Kern, Irving Berlin, George and Ira Gershwin, and Cole Porter decades earlier. So it is equally natural that McDonald and Mitchell have demonstrated their admiration for this repertoire in the years since they appeared in *Ragtime*—not only on stage but also in the recording studio.

For example, Audra McDonald released an album called *How Glory Goes* in 2000. The collection takes its name from a contemporary song by Broadway songwriter Adam Guettel, and it includes a few other recent compositions—including "Come Down from the Tree" from *Ragtime* songwriters Stephen Flaherty and Lynn Ahrens. About two-thirds of the album is dedicated to the American Songbook, however. McDonald shows her special affection for Harold Arlen and Johnny Mercer, offering her interpretations of songs like "Any Place I Hang My

Hat Is Home" and "The Man That Got Away." She even includes a beautiful rendition of Jerome Kern and Oscar Hammerstein's "Bill," which the pair wrote for *Show Boat* back in 1927.

McDonald performs the entire album with impressive musicality and expressive power. Her voice is both strong and subtle, and she imbues every phrase with meaning. As a result, the album sounds remarkably cohesive—a considerable feat given that her repertoire was written over the span of eight decades. This kind of unity is not entirely the result of McDonald's musical prowess, though; it would seem to require at least some musical similarities between the disparate songs. There are echoes of the past in the work of the contemporary songwriters represented, including a mostly consonant harmonic palette and patterns of repetition and contrast that accomplish much the same effect as the AABA form so often used in the American Songbook. Yet the more striking reality is not that the current composers and lyricists are indebted to their predecessors, but that the older songs sound as fresh and vibrant as the newer ones. They do not seem dated in any way. It is hard to imagine a listener distinguishing between the standards and the more recently composed material for any reason other than the familiarity of the former.

Of course, bringing these songs together in a single album also puts the contemporary selections in a position to be compared with the established classics. There is a kind of natural, positive association involved here, and it works remarkably well. For those listeners who already love the older repertoire, the newer songs show that such writing has not entirely disappeared—even if the results are not widely popularized with the general public. And, for those listeners who are simply fans of Audra McDonald, the selections from the American Songbook serve as a reminder that her career has been built not simply on contemporary productions but specifically on those uniquely indebted to the musical past in some way.

Admittedly, McDonald has a larger following among Broadway aficionados than with the general public, which makes her work in the recording studio less influential overall than, say, that of Tony Bennett. Still, she is one of the most widely visible Broadway performers of the past twenty years, appearing not only in theaters but also on television and even in the concert hall. As such, she has played an important role in keeping the American Songbook in the ears of many listeners today. And the same can be said for her *Ragtime* costar, Brian Stokes Mitchell.

Mitchell has also recorded an album with a mix of standards and contemporary Broadway selections. His self-titled *Brian Stokes Mitchell* (2006) is a compilation album featuring songs from the American Songbook such as "The Best Is Yet to Come" and "How Long Has This Been Going On?" alongside several tunes from Stephen Sondheim and, oddly enough, Adam Guettel's "How Glory Goes." In his choice of repertoire, then, he creates something very like McDonald's earlier album, one that emphasizes the connection between the American Songbook and contemporary Broadway. Yet Mitchell makes some more daring interpretive choices that challenge the listener to consider this relationship in more provocative ways. For one thing, he uses unusual arrangements—ones that experiment to varying degrees with rhythm, harmony, and instrumentation. This makes his performances remarkably fresh and interesting, but it also challenges the listener in a way that few performers outside the world of jazz have done. In fact, Mitchell acts and sounds more like a jazz artist here than a Broadway star, showcasing a wide range of interpretive options applicable to his chosen repertoire—both the standards and the contemporary favorites. Nowhere is this clearer than in his choice to merge Duke Ellington's "Take the 'A' Train" and Stephen Sondheim's "Another Hundred People" into a single track. To facilitate this, he capitalizes on the references to trains found in both sets of lyrics and sings them against an accompaniment that pieces together phrases from each song as though they are different cars being pulled by the same train engine. It is a tremendously creative piece of music, one that stretches both the listener and the songs themselves. It is a testament to the quality of these songs—not to mention Mitchell's musical ability—that they possess such flexibility.

The beauty of Mitchell's album is that it pushes the American Songbook forward. His performances here have no hint of nostalgia. Instead, he brings the past—both the long past and the recent past—together in a kind of postmodern musical collage, a collection of songs that sounds simultaneously familiar and avant-garde. Ironically, Mitchell released the album on the heels of two far more traditional projects—a 2000 revival of Cole Porter's *Kiss Me, Kate* for which he won a Tony Award and a 2005 concert version of the Rodgers and Hammerstein classic *South Pacific* at Carnegie Hall. Maybe Mitchell felt it was time to push the limits a bit more. Or perhaps he simply understands and appreciates the true plasticity of the American Songbook.

McDonald and Mitchell have continued to breathe new life into the popular standard and other Broadway repertoire in the past ten years. In an interesting historical twist, McDonald has recently appeared on Broadway as none other than Billie Holiday, performing selections Holiday helped popularize decades ago as well as some new dramatic songs written for the biographical production. Mitchell has issued a second solo album entitled *Simply Broadway* (2012), featuring some tracks from the American Songbook and some from more recent productions. And they are both scheduled to be part of a remarkable new staging of the 1921 musical *Shuffle Along*, a show staged by African Americans that proved enormously influential on popular music and culture in the age of the American Songbook. In all of these projects, Audra McDonald and Brian Stokes Mitchell demonstrate the richness of the popular standard in our contemporary culture. It is a vital link between the past and the present, one that seems to be at home in both times. It is also an important connection between different musical styles and interpretive approaches, reminding us that jazz, Broadway, and popular song are not actually as disparate as current marketing trends might suggest. And it is something that represents musical quality in the simplest sense—a foundation upon which new songwriters and new performers can and have built their own work.

MICHAEL BUBLÉ

Michael Bublé released his first album in 2003—a self-titled compilation of standards and modern popular hits. It was an enormous success, and it launched an internationally successful career for Bublé—one that has continued to give the American Songbook an amazing level of exposure. In fact, he has followed much the same formula for creating his subsequent albums, mixing popular standards and modern classics with what seems like relative ease.

In 2007, he released *Call Me Irresponsible*, which takes its name from the 1962 standard by Jimmy Van Heusen and Sammy Cahn. His rendition of the song swings hard by the conclusion—an approach that honors its heritage but also resonates especially well with contemporary listeners. After all, strong and vibrant rhythm continues to permeate the popular music landscape today, from blues-based rock to hip-hop and dance music. Bublé capitalizes on these kinds of broad similarities between the musical past and the musical present for the other standards on the album. His performance of Harold Arlen and Ted Koehler's "I've Got the World on a String," for example, swings with the sensibility of rhythm and blues in the 1950s rather than the soundscape of the 1930s when the song was written. This emphasizes the song's interpretive flexibility—its ability to move through time with variations in rhythmic flavor and overall sound while still retaining its essence. His version of Johnny Mercer's "Dream" comes the closest to sounding old-fashioned, with the dominance of strings and winds in the accompaniment and slow tempo. Yet even in this selection, Bublé speaks to the song's currency by simply emphasizing its lyrics. Mercer was a master of timeless wordsmithing, after all, and Bublé does his utmost not to get in the way.

Alongside such fresh interpretations of popular standards, Bublé offers his take on what we might call modern popular classics—songs that have the same kind of widespread cultural resonance and enduring popularity as standards, but that inhabit the minds of listeners as a specific rendition. These are songs from the latter half of the twentieth century, at which point the introduction of a new song by multiple artists had virtually disappeared from practice in the recording industry. Instead, it was a single performer's version that made its way to the top of the charts. All others came to be called "cover" versions, a name that depicts them as imitations and thus of lesser value.

With so much time passing between the original recordings of these songs and Bublé's adoption of them into his own repertoire, it is difficult to conceptualize his renditions as true cover versions. Some critics have used this language in describing them simply because it has become so common, but they actually share more artistically and culturally with his reinterpretations of selections from the American Songbook. In fact, his choice to perform these modern classics alongside more traditional standards makes a strong case that they actually possess some of the same musical qualities that, had they been written in an earlier time, might have made them standards rather than hits so strongly associated with a particular artist or group. This message is strengthened by Bublé's stylistic approach to the modern classics, which places them in the same sonic world as the rest of his offerings.

Consider, for instance, his performance of Eric Clapton's "Wonderful Tonight." In many ways, it is a perfect candidate for a standard-inspired interpretation. First, it is structured like a standard, with two statements of the same musical material followed by a contrasting bridge and another repeat of the opening material. Also, it is defined primarily by its melody. Clapton has written and performed many other songs more heavily defined by their instrumental sound and timbres. Perhaps the most famous example of this is "Sunshine of Your Love," which he did with Cream in the 1960s. "Wonderful Tonight," however, belongs to a later period in Clapton's career when he was not so deeply entrenched in an electrified, rock-oriented soundscape and became more interested in melody-driven songwriting. Lastly, the song's lyrics, while specific to the situation that inspired them, are timeless in their expression. As a result, it is not a far cry to perform the song as Bublé does. He partners with Brazilian Ivan Lins and the softer sounds of his accompanying orchestra to create something that honors Clapton as a composer rather than trying to emulate what only Clapton can do as a performer. To put it another way, he illuminates the standard, timeless qualities of what Clapton authored instead of trying to "cover" his original performance.

Bublé is thus making an effort to find material outside the American Songbook that might well be considered alongside it. He is drawing our attention to the fact that there may be more to the power of these modern classics than the talents of the performers who first popularized them. He obviously values songwriting as a craft, and he has found material worthy of his attention not only in the American Songbook—a collection he obviously loves—but also in some more recent artists as well.

Bublé's next album, *Crazy Love* (2009), only makes this clearer. Here, he chooses to combine the Hoagy Carmichael songs "Georgia on My Mind" and "Stardust" with the somewhat less-familiar standards "All I Do Is Dream of You" by Arthur Freed and Nacio Herb Brown and "All of Me" by Gerald Marks and Seymour Simons, as well as more recent classics like Don Henley's "Heartache Tonight" and Billy Vera's "At This Moment." These songs were written at different times by very different types of musicians, but Bublé highlights what they all share—

timeless messages, tuneful melodies, predictable structures, and the kind of musical meaning that transcends specific stylistic and interpretive choices.

ESPERANZA SPAULDING

Esperanza Spaulding is not a musician noted for being particularly traditional. In fact, innovative and eclectic are more appropriate words for her brand of jazz. Her range of influences spans the globe, and her tripartite role as vocalist, bassist, and composer is extremely rare. Yet she clearly knows the jazz that has preceded her, and like many other artists who lean toward the avant-garde, she has made it a part of her creative palette.

For example, her 2008 debut album includes a Spanish-language rendition of Johnny Green's "Body and Soul"—"Cuerpo y Alma." Her take on the song is recognizable but also remarkably original. She sings the same melody as Billie Holiday, but Spaulding's interpretation is that of a lover who feels freed by romance rather than plagued by it. In part, this stems from Spaulding's resetting of the melody against a five-beat meter instead of the original—and far more familiar—four-beat meter. Because most American listeners' ears are not accustomed to five-beat groupings, the result feels flexible and continuous, even bouncy, rather than fixed and formulaic. In addition, Spaulding's voice simply sounds happy to give her all—her body and soul—to the one she loves. She sings with a lightness and playfulness that exude positive energy. In short, the message of her rendition is very different from that of Billie Holiday.

And yet, her choice to revisit this particular song acknowledges and honors its iconic place in the jazz standard repertoire. It is her tribute to the artists who have given it this place, and she demonstrates her understanding of what they have done even as she creates her own original version. Even though she sounds very different from Billie Holiday, both vocally and emotionally, the strength of her communicative ability as a musician matches that of her predecessor. Like Holiday, she has a remarkable sense of timing as a singer. As the bassist, she creates the underlying rhythms of the song with great precision, yet her voice seems to operate with the same kind of independence we hear in many of Holiday's recordings. It is deeply connected to its roots yet also free to move on its own. Similarly, the harmonic adventurousness of her interpretation evokes the celebrated recording from Coleman Hawkins without mimicking it in any way. There is nothing that overtly references Hawkins, but the spirit of what he created—including musical fluidity and harmonic ingenuity—is very much present.

Spaulding's rendition is thus another reminder of how the American Songbook continues to permeate the contemporary musical landscape, especially in the world of jazz. And her innovative voice makes this presence especially powerful. For her, "Body and Soul" is hardly a song that belongs in the past but instead a vibrant piece of music that remains meaningful and inspirational. In many ways, it offers performers like Spaulding the same basis for creative expression that it did to those living in earlier decades.

It is worth noting that Spaulding's integration of the American Songbook into her catalog does not have the same comparative effect as most other albums that mix together this repertoire with others. Here, the suggestion is not that the new songs included are to be considered standards like "Body and Soul," but rather that she is simply performing a standard to show her familiarity with the jazz repertoire and her ability to reinterpret it with her own creative voice. The reason for this is simply the original nature of the material she offers along with "Body and Soul." The album is not a sequence of songs from various points in history; it is almost exclusively her composition and improvisation—with a time-honored melody thrown in for good measure.

WALL-E

Hollywood has continued to nurture the standard repertoire in numerous ways, but perhaps nowhere more prominently than in its animated films. This type of film seems especially conducive to song, and while many animated films of the past ten years have included entirely new scores, others have incorporated older songs as well. Pixar's WALL-E from 2008 is a clear and beautiful example of how selections from the American Songbook performed by artists from the first half of the twentieth century have continued to resonate with contemporary audiences.

The context of the film provides an ideal backdrop for the addition of songs from a different time. It takes place in the future, when the Earth has become uninhabitable after too much abuse by humanity. The people have taken up residence on a spaceship, leaving trash-compacting robots identified by the acronym WALL-E (Waste Allocation Load Lifter—Earth-class) to clean up their mess and return the planet to a state that can support life. One of these robots serves as the protagonist in the story, and the film begins by following him around as he extracts the objects he finds most meaningful from the rest of the things the humans have tossed out.

Among these is a VHS tape recording of the film *Hello, Dolly*— which he plays regularly and seems to find mesmerizing. He is especially drawn to the song "It Only Takes a Moment," in which two of the characters sing about their romantic attachment—one that, as the song suggests, can last a "whole life long." What intrigues him the most is when the characters hold hands at the climax of the melody—something that is deeply human. WALL-E wants to understand and experience this, which is why he tries to re-create it by clasping his own hands together. But, of course, this does not create the same effect he sees in the film because he is not connecting with another creature.

Fortunately, he sees the opportunity to experience this a bit later in the film when he meets EVE (Extraterrestrial Vegetation Evaluator)— another type of robot who has been sent back to Earth to determine if it can support life again. WALL-E is immediately taken with EVE, so much so that he tries to befriend her even though she begins their first encounter by shooting at him. He even shows her his collection, including the video recording of "It Only Takes a Moment," at which point he tries unsuccessfully to hold her hand.

WALL-E ends up following EVE back into space and engaging on an adventurous series of events that not only brings the two of them together but also brings their human friends back home. As things proceed, EVE is increasingly drawn to WALL-E's unending dedication to her. Near the end of the film, when WALL-E seems to be injured beyond repair, the touch of EVE's hand—beautifully coordinated with another iteration of "It Only Takes a Moment"—brings him back to life. Here, the audience sees very clearly just how human these robots have become.

Significantly, music is an important part of that transformation. Jerry Herman's song does more than accompany the action here; it represents something innately human that humans have nevertheless left behind. As a result, composer Thomas Newman's choice to use a song like "It Only Takes a Moment" seems especially poignant. It contributes to the nostalgia of the film in a very special way—as something that belongs to and reminds us of the past but still retains tremendous currency. To put it another way, the film articulates the timeless nature of the American Songbook with remarkable clarity—even if it does so unconsciously.

Of course, by simply including the song in his score, Newman keeps it in the present for his audience. He is making it a part of contemporary popular culture even as he honors its place in history. And this is especially important given the target audience for the film—children born decades after *Hello, Dolly!* first appeared on Broadway or on film. Indeed, many of the parents of the children for whom the film was written would not have been part of the musical's original audience. Some may know it because they enjoy film musicals or the American Songbook more generally, but not because they experienced the show in its heyday. As such, Newman is giving this classic song an important layer of exposure—one that has made it fresh in the ears of contemporary listeners.

HARRY CONNICK JR. AND DIANA KRALL

Harry Connick Jr. and Diana Krall have remained important figures in the contemporary life of the American Songbook. In fact, 2009 saw the release of new albums featuring this repertoire from each of these artists. Connick's *Your Songs* and Krall's *Quiet Nights* are both compilation albums of both traditional standards and modern popular classics, echoing the approach of numerous others who have combined the American Songbook with more recent material. Yet Connick and Krall each do this in distinctive ways, offering listeners their own unique take on both repertoires. And, in so doing, they also showcase the versatility of these songs—both the standards and the modern classics.

On his website, Connick shares some of the creative process that went into making *Your Songs*. This includes his role in choosing the tracks, a task he shared with his longtime producer, Clive Davis. They include standards such as "The Way You Look Tonight," "Smile," and "All the Way," as well as the work of more recent songwriters such as Billy Joel's "Just the Way You Are" and the John Lennon/Paul McCartney favorite, "And I Love Her." Notably, though, his approach to interpreting all of the songs is essentially the same—one that dates back to the age of the American Songbook, when songs were defined by their melody and lyrics rather than a specific recorded performance. "Although I have wrestled with this for some time," Connick writes, "I don't think that anyone's version of a great song, however classic, should preclude my singing it. . . . I take each song in its rawest form, as it appears on the sheet music, and go from there." To think of contemporary pop songs in this way—as something that ultimately comes from sheet music—has not been very common in recent years, though the idea is making a comeback thanks to Connick and others who have revisited it. His appearance as a judge on *American Idol*, a talent show where unknown performers offer new interpretations of all kinds of popular songs, has only extended the public's familiarity with and acceptance of this traditional approach to music making.

Connick also took the lead in arranging the songs, combining his big band forces with a larger string orchestra—something he has done on other occasions as well, though perhaps not as often as he would have liked. "I have never really been able to do that kind of writing throughout an entire record," he writes. "It's a more spacious approach, with the orchestra in service to the singing; and it was a kick to sing over those charts." To put it another way, Connick wrote his arrangements to emphasize the melody, another way in which the album hearkens back to an earlier era of popular music.

Of course, Connick's most defining contribution is his singing, which he does with what he calls a "straight" approach to the melodies. This "can be deceptively hard," he adds, but it is what makes his interpretations so rich, so vibrant, and so deeply indebted to the songs themselves. He truly honors these songs as compositions—ones that do not belong to any person or any time but to American popular culture as a whole.

Diana Krall's *Quiet Nights* is different in flavor yet similar in substance to Connick's work that same year. Her decision to feature several Brazilian-authored songs—including "The Girl from Ipanema"—ultimately infused the album as a whole with a Latin feel. For example, her rendition of the Rodgers and Hart classic "Where or When" sets the familiar melody against a bossa nova rhythm in the accompaniment. This distinguishes the album from much of her earlier work—and from many other interpretations of the American Songbook—on a purely stylistic level. Yet, like Connick, Krall is not just interested in bringing fresh interpretive ideas to this repertoire or even in crossing the boundaries between jazz, Latin, and popular music. She is also striving to reposition more contemporary songs as popular standards. In this case, she offers a performance of Burt Bacharach's "Walk on By" in much the same style as all of the other songs on the album. Like Connick, then, she is approaching Bacharach's song in its rawest form, embracing an approach to interpretation that is rooted in an earlier era of songwriting and song performance.

Connick and Krall probably come to this approach fairly easily because they inhabit the world of jazz—a place where even the most iconic and influential recordings rarely displace the song as a template for interpretation, improvisation, and overall creative expression. In fact, jazz musicians have long used not only standards but virtually all composed material both freely and flexibly, without any sense that a song exists in a single definitive form. Yet their specific inclination toward the American Songbook seems to be an equally strong influence in the way they choose to look at the musical material they interpret. The way in which this repertoire is so melodically defined naturally inspires a mode of performance where all other elements are arranged around it. To put it another way, the way these songs are written makes it easy to reinvent them without losing their essence. Clearly, both Connick and Krall see these traits in the more recent songs they also choose to perform, which only suggests that songwriting techniques of Irving Berlin and Cole Porter may not be as far removed from contemporary popular culture as we might think.

TONY BENNETT

Tony Bennett has built what seems like a new career for himself in the past decade. To be sure, he is singing the same material in much the same way. He is perhaps an even more clearly defined version of his younger self, something that often comes with age and artistic maturity. By introducing himself to a new generation of listeners, however, he has revived not only his own career but also the kind of music to which he has been dedicated for his entire life.

This trajectory began with *Duets: An American Classic* in 2006, when he paired with a wide variety of well-known recording artists to record a wealth of popular standards and a handful of modern classics. Some of his partners, such as Barbra Streisand, Diana Krall, and Michael Bublé, are not all that surprising given their established connection to the repertoire of the American Songbook and Bennett's basic style of singing. In other cases, though, he purposely stretched beyond his own musical realm to perform with country singers like Tim McGraw and the Dixie Chicks, as well as mainstay rock personalities like Paul McCartney, Sting, and Bono. One reason for this stretch was almost certainly the public relations potential; unusual and unexpected musical pairings usually attract attention and, by extension, help to sell records. On the other hand, though, it also offered Bennett a chance to record the songs he loves with other singers who, despite their typical labels, actually have something in their musicality that makes them well-suited to the popular standard. Sting, for instance, grew up playing bass in jazz ensembles before he broke out as a rock artist as the leading man of the Police—an experience that surely familiarized him with numerous standards. Many of Paul McCartney's songs follow some sort of AABA pattern, which he no doubt absorbed from the pre-rock era in popular music. And, by partnering with Tim McGraw to sing "Cold, Cold Heart," Bennett brings his own connection with this classic from the country repertoire full circle. Bennett recorded the Hank Williams number early in his career, not as an attempt at "crossover" but simply in recognition of the song's inherent timelessness—something that has proven to be the case.

In this sense, Bennett's project makes yet another strong statement about the nature of the popular standard as it exists today. Like Michael Bublé, Harry Connick Jr., and Diana Krall, Bennett is—at least to some extent—modifying the definition of the American Songbook to encompass songs with many of the same essential musical qualities, even if they have been written at a different point in history or introduced in a different style. By bringing such diverse collaborators into the picture, he is also emphasizing the reasons songs were written this way in the first place. After all, the purpose of the American Songbook in its own time was to be interpreted in a wide variety of ways by a wide variety of artists for a mass of listeners.

Several years passed before Bennett released the sequel to this project, entitled simply *Duets II*. When he did so, he found an unexpectedly well-suited partner in Lady Gaga. Their initial collaboration on the Rodgers and Hart favorite "The Lady Is a Tramp" for *Duets II* ultimately led to another complete album featuring the unlikely duo: the traditional crooner in his eighties and the unconventional diva of contemporary pop culture sixty years his junior. Taking its name from the Irving Berlin classic "Cheek to Cheek," their expanded collaboration was released three years later in 2014, featuring an array of standards including "I Won't Dance," "It Don't Mean a Thing," and "Anything Goes."

Needless to say, Bennett's work with Lady Gaga has made him a household name with multitudes of young listeners. More importantly, though, their partnership has made these songs part of the pop music vernacular once again—and not just because Lady Gaga's name and image appear on the album. She sings this repertoire with a blend of tradition and freshness that coordinates beautifully with Bennett's own historical standing and his seemingly never-ending energy. She sounds very much at home with the repertoire, with a voice that evokes the powerful stage presence of Ethel Merman, the vocal artistry of Ella Fitzgerald, and the solid simplicity of Helen Forrest—all in a contemporary package. To put it another way, her performances are genuine in every way. And, when complemented by Bennett's own singing, the result is truly music for the masses.

Bennett could easily have made his collaboration with Lady Gaga the endcap to his career, but he shows no signs of stopping. Just one year later in 2015, he released an album of Jerome Kern songs with pianist Bill Charlap entitled *The Silver Lining*—a title inspired by none other than Kern's "Look for the Silver Lining" from the 1919 stage production of *Sally*. The compilation makes an interesting follow-up to *Cheek to Cheek*—one that seems like a conscious effort to capitalize on his recently established name recognition with American youth and pull them more deeply into the world in which the American Songbook was born. Even though his work with Lady Gaga is very much rooted in tradition, his choices here are more strongly connected to the history of the repertoire. For one thing, he exclusively presents songs from a single composer—an echo of Ella Fitzgerald's albums devoted to indi-vidual contributors to the American Songbook. Not only that, he chooses one of the oldest and most revered composers from the catalog, one whose songwriting influenced and shaped the work of many who followed in his footsteps. In addition, he chooses a jazz musician as his collaborator, one who approaches this material in a largely conventional manner; like many of his predecessors, Charlap offers his own original touch while still honoring the melodies as they were composed. And finally, he employs the simplest and most traditional of arrangements—just voice and piano. All of this reminds the listener of how these songs originated, from their compositional quality to their relationship to jazz and their interpretive flexibility.

Time will tell whether Bennett's efforts on this particular album will have a significant impact on the listeners who have followed his more market-friendly collaborations—whether it will sell widely on Bennett's name alone and plunge young audiences deeper into the history of the American Songbook. But, even if its effects are modest, Bennett will still have introduced these songs to millions of young ears. And he will have convinced many such ears to keep listening as more and more singers add them to their catalog.

THE AMERICAN SONGBOOK ON RADIO AND TELEVISION

Admittedly, radio and television are not playing as large of a role in the distribution of music as they once were. In the 1920s and 1930s, radio was a popular and relatively inexpensive source of musical entertain-ment for people all over the country. Various radio shows were devel-oped, each showcasing the newest and most celebrated artists involved in a particular type of music. Listeners could simply tune in to hear live performances of their favorite music in the comfort of their own homes. Then, as television became an equally affordable and common technol-ogy in the 1950s, music programming similar to that heard on radio stations was featured prominently—only now audiences could see as well as hear the performers. From *American Bandstand* to *The Law-rence Welk Show*, musical programs featuring live performance were widely popular.

Since the advent of digital recording and the Internet, both radio and television have focused more on non-musical programs. The musical programming that remains is largely of a different kind. Radio, for instance, has turned almost exclusively to recorded music rather than live performance. This situates radio as an extension of the recording industry—a place where listeners can hear the recordings with which they are already familiar and those new ones they might wish to purchase. Television, on the other hand, continues to include live performances, but most of them differ from the musical variety shows of the twentieth century in one of two ways. Many of those featured on major networks in recent years have generally involved a competitive component, such as *American Idol*, *The Voice*, and *America's Got Talent*. Conversely, those aired on public broadcasting stations have featured classical music and jazz more often than contemporary popular styles.

Still, the American Songbook has permeated all of these avenues to a much greater extent than one might expect for a musical repertoire approaching the century mark in age. Radio listeners can tune into Dick Robinson's *American Standards by the Sea* program and hear their favorite recordings of this repertoire, either via traditional radio or online. Subscribers to Sirius XM can find stations devoted to standards, including *Siriusly Sinatra* and *40s Junction*. And, of course, artists like Michael Bublé can be heard on a wide variety of stations, albeit with less regularity. Standards have also been heard on television shows like *American Idol*, not only by invited guests already associated with the repertoire—including none other than Tony Bennett—but also by the aspiring artists themselves. And PBS has aired a number of programs related to the American Songbook, ranging from Michael Feinstein's documentary-style series on the subject to contemporary performances of Rodgers and Hammerstein musicals like *Oklahoma!* and *South Pacific*.

These sprinklings of the American Songbook into the contemporary world of radio and television might not seem like much—especially compared to the way in which they once dominated the airwaves. But because music is a smaller portion of both radio and television programming today and most of the music featured is new, the fact that the American Songbook has any presence there at all speaks to its endurance and its relevance for contemporary listeners. Clearly, it has not been forgotten—and it does not look like it will be anytime soon.

THE AMERICAN SONGBOOK IN PRINT

In addition to the myriad ways in which the American Songbook has been heard in recent years, a number of books on the subject have also been written—ones that range widely in approach and focus yet collectively illuminate the same musical repertoire. In 2015 alone, Dominic Symonds published his first of two books on the work of Richard Rodgers and Lorenz Hart; Andy Probst and Walter Rimler have released much-needed biographies of Cy Coleman and Harold Arlen, respectively; Ben Yagoda has contributed an insightful volume of how the business of music has shaped the history of the American Songbook; and Philip Furia has offered another tome—partnering this time with Laurie J. Patterson—chronicling the history of individual songs in the collection. Clearly, the topic is a pertinent one for all kinds of readers.

To be sure, there has been a vast increase in scholarship on popular music—as well as popular culture more generally—over the past twenty-five years or so. After years of neglect, historians in a variety of disciplines have begun to recognize the value of studying such things. To some extent, the aforementioned books are just one small part of this broader trend. Still, two of these come not from professional historians or scholars but from journalists. This not only makes for a book with a different kind of tone; it also suggests that these authors were motivated by something beyond a desire to fill in the gaps in the history of music and theater scholarship. As journalists, they are immediately connected to the American public and its interests. As such, their work is built on—and seemingly inspired by—the increasingly widespread interest in the American Songbook with the masses in recent years.

To put it another way, the appearance of books like these is yet another testament to how the American Songbook seems to be reclaiming its original place within American popular culture. It is once again becoming music for the masses—music for the old and for the young, music for the traditionalist and for the experimentalist, and now, music of the past and of the present. This is no small feat given the changes in recording technology, musical ideology, and marketplace practices that have transpired over the past century. Yet the timelessness of the material has enabled it to endure.

EPILOGUE

Amateurs and the American Songbook

The history of the American Songbook is filled with people who have dedicated their professional lives to creating, interpreting, recording, and selling this repertoire. It is also filled with countless amateur musicians who have contributed not only to the widespread familiarity of these songs but also their integration into everyday life and their place in the American consciousness. Community choirs, bands, and theater troupes perform them. Students sing and play them in concerts and stage productions. They are rendered by everyday people at all kinds of celebrations, from the personal to the patriotic. In short, there are many individuals and ensembles around the country that, whether regularly or occasionally, make this repertoire a part of what they do.

Amateurs have thus continued to proliferate what the professionals have introduced and, in so doing, have helped situate these songs in everyday life. Their renditions remind us that these songs are not only to be heard by the masses; they are also to be sung and played by them. Their renderings might or might not be memorable to anyone but themselves and their immediate communities, but their very involvement in re-creating them is part of what has embedded these songs so deeply into American popular culture.

This widespread involvement of amateur musicians makes the American Songbook unique among the various subcategories of popular music. Amateurs are not absent in the histories of other popular styles, of course, but nowhere else have they played such a significant role in actually disseminating and sharing the music. In other genres, they are generally viewed as imitators of the original. In the performance of standards, however, they have become additional performers of a common repertoire.

To those readers who are also amateur performers, I hope you will both recognize and relish your special role in the history of these songs. I hope you will remember the people who first introduced them to you. And I hope you will continue to share them with your own community—especially the next generation. After all, these are truly songs for everyone. They are music for the masses.

FURTHER READING

There are many, many books that pertain to the American Songbook in some way. A large number of these are biographical in nature, focusing on a particular singer, instrumentalist, composer, or lyricist whose work contributed to the repertoire. Others focus on a particular part of the entertainment industry that pertains to the American Songbook, such as Broadway, Hollywood, or jazz. And, of course, there are some that use the song collection as their subject. Those listed here are ones that most closely complement this book—ones that allow the reader interested in specific musical issues raised here to explore them in more detail.

Bordman, Gerald. *Jerome Kern: His Life and Music*. New York: Oxford University Press, 1990. Gerald Bordman's time-honored biography of Jerome Kern remains an important resource for anyone interested in Kern's work. Because Bordman writes with a focus on that work, there is a wealth of information on both the cultural environment and the entertainment industry of which he was a part. In short, if you are looking for a book pertaining to the early history of the American Songbook, you will find it here.

Dregni, Michael. *Django: The Life and Music of a Gypsy Legend*. New York: Oxford University Press, 2004. Though there are many performer biographies related to the American Songbook, I have only chosen to include this one on Django Reinhardt here. The reason is that Dregni's book illuminates not just a single interpreter but an entire musical sphere. After all, Reinhardt's life and music are themselves a fascinating study in the mixing of musical cultures—Romani, French, and American—and a particularly interesting example of how the popular standard has transcended the time and place that gave it birth.

Fordin, Hugh. *MGM's Greatest Musicals: The Arthur Freed Unit*. New York: Da Capo Press, 1996. Hugh Fordin's look at the career of Arthur Freed provides an interesting glimpse into the world of the film musical. His is not a scholarly analysis of these films but rather a historical account of how they were developed and the performers and songwriters who worked with Freed to make them happen. His book is thus a welcome resource for those interested in how various creative talents came together to forge some of the most celebrated film musicals of all time.

Furia, Philip. *Skylark: The Life and Times of Johnny Mercer*. New York: St. Martin's Press, 2003. Philip Furia is a familiar name to anyone interested in the American Songbook, as he has authored or co-authored a number of books on individual songwriters as well as the collection as a whole. In this particular volume, he offers readers his knowledge of songwriter Johnny Mercer. His biography is fairly comprehensive, giving equal attention to both Mercer's private life and his professional work. Even though all of the information in the former category may not be relevant to every reader, some of it does help set the stage for how and why Mercer wrote as he did. So, like Bordman's biography of Jerome Kern, the book as a whole provides a sense of the circumstances that nurtured the American Songbook—in this case, as the middle of the twentieth century approached.

Furia, Philip, and Michael Lasser. *America's Songs: The Stories behind the Songs of Broadway, Hollywood, and Tin Pan Alley*. New York: Routledge, 2006. Here, Philip Furia partners with Michael Lasser to provide a series of brief articles on numerous selections from the American Songbook. Because it is organized in this encyclopedic fashion, it makes a particularly useful resource for anyone looking into the history of a specific song. The overall coverage of songs is impressively broad, though the entries themselves could go deeper—especially with respect to musical details. It is nevertheless a good place to find basic information.

Furia, Philip, and Laurie J. Patterson. *The American Song Book: The Tin Pan Alley Era*. New York: Oxford University Press, 2015. Furia's latest effort with Laurie J. Patterson is an expansion of his earlier volume with Michael Lasser. This book is still a series of essays on individual songs, but each essay here is more extensive—more like a full chapter rather than an encyclopedic entry. Also, Furia and Patterson include musical scores with their discussion, allowing for a bit more musical detail in the accompanying prose. Still, their focus is on the cultural history and lyrical expression in these songs rather than their musical content. Readers looking for specific information of this type on individual songs discussed here will naturally find it useful.

Gioia, Ted. *The History of Jazz*. New York: Oxford University Press, 2011. Ted Gioia's history of jazz offers an accessible yet detailed history of the genre. For readers interested in exploring how the histories of jazz and the American Songbook are intertwined, Gioia's book is a reliable and interesting place to start. Of course, the American Songbook is not at the forefront here, but it makes mention of numerous songs, composers, and performers that figure prominently in these overlapping repertoires. Perhaps more importantly, Gioia's book provides a rich look into issues such as racial and national identity and musical philosophy that affect not only the respective histories of both jazz and the American Songbook but also the ways in which they have interacted over the years.

Gioia, Ted. *The Jazz Standards: A Guide to the Repertoire*. New York: Oxford University Press, 2012. Gioia's book on jazz standards is an easy-to-navigate source with brief histories of numerous standards. In this respect, it is very similar in structure to Philip Furia and Michael Lasser's *America's Songs: The Stories behind the Songs of Broadway, Hollywood, and Tin Pan Alley*. Gioia's book differs in two key ways, however. First, his target reader is the jazz performer. As such, he provides not only general historical information about each song but also useful information for performers, such as musical descriptions and recommended recordings from prominent artists in jazz history. Second, the "standard" repertoire he covers is the one used in the jazz world today, which overlaps significantly with but is not exactly the same as the American Songbook. For instance, he includes a number of songs widely performed in jazz that are neither culturally nor musically related to the songs discussed here. Conversely, he also understandably omits selections from the American Songbook that have been less frequently interpreted by jazz musicians.

Hasse, John Edward. *Beyond Category: The Life and Genius of Duke Ellington*. New York: Da Capo Press, 1993. John Edward Hasse has served as Curator of American Music of the Smithsonian Institution for many years, and his biography of Duke Ellington is noted as the first one based on the large Ellington archive within its collections. He also produced and annotated a companion set of archival recordings for the book, appropriate titled

Beyond Category. Hasse takes a scholarly yet accessible approach to his writing, resulting in a useful resource for almost anyone interested in Ellington and his music.

Hasse, John Edward. *Beyond Category: The Life and Genius of Duke Ellington*. New York: Da Capo Press, 1995. Despite their lasting influence as part of the American Songbook, Duke Ellington's songs rarely receive what seems like the kind of attention they deserve in accounts of his life and work. Of course, Ellington's musical life is so varied and his accomplishments are so noteworthy that it makes it difficult for any biographer to adequately emphasize everything he did. John Edward Hasse does an excellent job of representing Ellington's songs within his larger narrative, however, and he does so in a voice that is remarkably accessible. His "Essential Ellington" tidbits are especially valuable. If you want a solid, insightful, and musically oriented study of Duke Ellington, you will find it here.

Jablonski, Edward. *Gershwin: A Biography*. New York: Doubleday, 1987. Numerous biographies of George Gershwin have been written since Edward Jablonski penned his in 1987. Still, it remains an essential source of information on the songwriter and his work. His writing is accessible yet full of key details on the music of this important and influential composer.

Katz, Mark. *Capturing Sound: How Technology Has Changed Music*. Berkeley: University of California Press, 2004. Mark Katz is a widely respected music scholar who, in this book, offers his readers an opportunity to explore the many ways music technology has affected music—from the ways it is written and performed to the ways it is consumed and categorized. Though the American Songbook is not central to his topic, his first chapter provides an excellent introduction to aspects of recorded music such as repeatability, portability, and temporality—all of which have profoundly shaped the life of the American Songbook. We who have never known a world without recorded music tend to forget about the significance of these things—if we have thought about them in the first place. Readers interested in the role of recording technology in the history of the American Songbook will undoubtedly find Katz's book illuminating.

Kenney, William Howland. *Recorded Music in American Life: The Phonograph and Popular Memory, 1890–1945*. New York: Oxford University Press, 1999. Kenney's collection of essays on the relationship between recorded music and American culture will provide curious readers with more information on the myriad ways in which recorded music and American culture influenced each other in the early twentieth century. Several of the essays focus on the recording and distribution of nonmainstream musical styles during the early twentieth century, those that—in contrast to the American Songbook—were marketed to specific demographic groups. The final two, however, are more pertinent to the popular standard. Their titles, "A Renewed Flow of Memories: The Depression and the Struggle over 'Hit Records'" and "Popular Recorded Music within the Context of National Life," point to the academic tone of Kenney's writing. The book is not technical on a musical level, however, making it approachable for anyone interested in this kind of sociological study.

Magee, Jeffrey. *Irving Berlin's American Musical Theater*. New York: Oxford University Press, 2012. Despite its seemingly focused title, this book covers a much wider swath of Irving Berlin's work than most readers might suppose. This is because Berlin played a much bigger role in the development of American musical theater than is often recognized—something Jeffrey Magee makes abundantly clear here. As he uncovers Berlin's rich contributions to Broadway history, he enlightens his readers with fascinating new research on even his more familiar, beloved songs. The text is scholarly in nature, with particular attention given to musical issues. Still, it is not so erudite that more casual readers will be turned away.

McMillin, Scott. *The Musical as Drama*. Princeton: Princeton University Press, 2006. Scott McMillin's book is a landmark piece of scholarship on the history of musical theater in the United States. In it, he argues that the introduction of more dramatically interesting stories to the musical stage led to the development and use of more dramatically relevant music, and he looks at a number of celebrated stage productions from the mid-twentieth century to make his point. Because his work has such a nuanced focus, it is likely more interesting to academics and specialists than to a general readership. Nevertheless, the style is approachable enough for anyone who wants to know more about the rise of the so-called "integrated" musical.

Pollack, Howard. *George Gershwin: His Life and Work*. Berkeley: University of California Press, 2007. There is no more comprehensive biography of George Gershwin available than this one by Howard Pollack. In fact, the breadth and depth of the research here is so compelling that it is hard to imagine a more extensive volume on the composer could even be written. As a result, Pollack's discussion of Gershwin's songs is unparalleled in its level of detail. As a musicologist, his writing tends to cater toward the scholarly audience, though much of it is certainly accessible to the more casual Gershwin fan.

Rosen, Jody. *White Christmas: The Story of an American Song*. New York: Scribner, 2007. It is rare for a book to tell the story of a single song, but Irving Berlin's "White Christmas" is so richly embedded in our popular culture that it actually warrants this kind of attention. Jody Rosen has created a lovely narrative of the song's history that will prove interesting to almost any reader. It is more socially oriented than musically detailed but will provide everyone with thought-provoking information on this influential song.

Sears, Benjamin, ed. *The Irving Berlin Reader*. New York, Oxford University Press, 2012. Benjamin Sears is a devoted interpreter of the American Songbook, so he brings a performer's sensibility to his research and writing. Here, he presents an eclectic mix of material about Irving Berlin, ranging from portions of major scholarly studies on the songwriter to recollections from Berlin's professional peers, reviews of his work printed in the mainstream press, and some of his own published words. Sears has arranged them in a rough chronology, not according to their own dates of composition but rather how they pertain to Berlin's life. The result is an informative collection that touches on a wide range of topics yet still reads nicely, and almost biographically, from beginning to end. For anyone interested in the songs of Irving Berlin, this book is an excellent resource.

Sudhalter, Richard M. *Stardust Melody: The Life and Music of Hoagy Carmichael*. New York: Oxford University Press, 2003. Richard Sudhalter's biography of Hoagy Carmichael is similar in scope and overall approach to the others listed here. While it naturally contains information on Carmichael's private life, the focus is on his professional work—including plenty of musical commentary and analysis. Like Benjamin Sears, Sudhalter brings his own sensibility as an interpreter of the American Songbook to his writing. This makes his admiration for Carmichael especially compelling and his insights into his songs all the more valuable. Moreover, jazz fans will appreciate the richness with which he explores Carmichael's place in the genre.

Teachout, Terry. *Duke: A Life of Duke Ellington*. New York: Gotham Books, 2013. Teachout's biography of Duke Ellington is one of the more recent to have emerged on the bookshelf. It is an easy and flavorful read, reflecting Teachout's years of experience writing liner notes and serving as drama critic for the *Wall Street Journal*. Overall, it provides a solid, thought-provoking look at Ellington's life and work.

Wilder, Alec. *American Popular Song: The Great Innovators, 1900–1950*. New York: Oxford University Press, 1972. Alec Wilder's book is a seminal piece of popular music history. Despite its age, it remains a relevant source for anyone interested in the nature of popular songwriting. Wilder writes as a composer who admires the skill of his predecessors, and he includes plenty of musical evidence for his conclusions. He therefore mixes his opinions with more objective observations, but not in a way that makes them indistinguishable from one another.

Yagoda, Ben. *The B Side: The Death of Tin Pan Alley and the Rebirth of the Great American Song*. New York: Riverhead Books, 2015. Yagoda's book follows a similar historical trajectory to this one, but with one major difference: he focuses on how the business of music shaped the decline of the American Songbook in the 1950s and 1960s. Yagoda brings a wealth of commercial and marketing details into play, all of which is a fascinating complement to the broader cultural shifts explored here. His approach to research is journalistic, as is his writing style. All of this makes for an engaging read that further explains how the stylistic introduction of rock and roll was only a small piece of a much larger music industry puzzle that pushed standards out of the limelight for a while.

FURTHER LISTENING

Creating a comprehensive list of the recordings for the American Songbook would be a daunting, almost impossible task. The following is therefore intended to be a diverse sampling of offerings featuring some of the more prominent artists discussed in this book who have recorded this repertoire.

FRED ASTAIRE

The Astaire Story (December 1952), album, Verve Records. Fred Astaire was a star of stage and screen—not a recording artist. Still, he took the opportunity to go into the studio with no less a collaborator than jazz pianist Oscar Peterson to record many of the songs he had helped popularize through other media. The album showcases Astaire's voice for what it was—clear, warm, and rhythmically vital. These qualities coordinate well with the jazz sensibilities that dominate the album as a whole, even if Astaire's voice does not have the same power as singers more rooted in jazz. Of course, the very production of an album like this speaks volumes about the relationship between jazz and the American Songbook in the 1950s.

Fred Astaire: Early Years at RKO (November 2013), two-CD set, Sony Masterworks. If you are looking for audio recordings that capture what Astaire produced on film, this compilation provides them. Released in conjunction with Turner Classic Movies, it contains many of the songs most associated with Astaire including "Cheek to Cheek," "The Way You Look Tonight," "Top Hat, White Tie and Tails," and "Night and Day."

COUNT BASIE

Sinatra-Basie: An Historic Musical First (December 1962), album, Reprise. This album brings together two of the greatest musical talents associated with the American Songbook—Frank Sinatra and Count Basie. Sinatra's previous hits figure prominently, with recordings of "Pennies from Heaven," "The Tender Trap," "Nice Work If You Can Get It," and "Learnin' the Blues."

Count Basie's Finest Hour (May 2002), CD, Verve. This collection follows Basie's recording career from the 1930s to the 1960s. In addition to Basie specials like "One O'Clock Jump" and "Topsy," it includes his celebrated renditions of standards like "April in Paris" and "All of Me."

Basie Swings Standards (March 2009), CD, Pablo. This disc is a compilation of later Count Basie recordings from the 1970s. It includes performances of songs such as "Satin Doll," "On the Sunny Side of the Street," "Strike Up the Band," and "In a Mellow Tone."

TONY BENNETT

Duets: An American Classic (September 2006), album, Sony. This collaborative album is the first of several in Bennett's recent output. Collectively, they demonstrate his efforts to revive the notion of the standard as something for any type of singer—not just something for singers of a certain style or era. To make this point, he purposely chooses a wide range of collaborators and material, drawing attention to the way in which we define the standard as well as the body of artists who interpret them.

The Essential Tony Bennett (September 2009), two-CD set, Sony. This compilation offers a nice overview of Bennett's long career as an interpreter of standards. While some selections are familiar favorites from outside the American Songbook—such as Hank Williams's "Cold, Cold, Heart"—the collection as a whole contains a solid representation of the repertoire including "The Very Thought of You," "Night and Day," "The Shadow of Your Smile," "It Don't Mean a Thing If It Ain't Got That Swing," and "The Best Is Yet to Come." It also offers listeners a chance to hear Bennett develop over time, from his early successes in the 1950s to the more recent past.

Duets II (September 2011), album, Columbia. In this follow-up to *Duets: An American Classic*, Bennett continues to challenge any suggestion that the American standard is in any way outdated. His collaborators for this album are mostly very young—not just younger than Bennett, but true newcomers to the popular music scene.

Cheek to Cheek (September 2014), album, Streamline/Columbia/Interscope. Bennett's collaboration with Lady Gaga on *Duets II* led to a complete album featuring the pair of singers. In addition to the title track, the album includes such standards as "Anything Goes," "I Won't Dance," "Let's Face the Music and Dance," and "It Don't Mean a Thing If It Ain't Got That Swing."

The Silver Lining: The Songs of Jerome Kern (September 2015), album, Columbia. After several years of partnering with other pop singers to keep the American Songbook in the public ear, Bennett has most recently turned to jazz pianist Bill Charlap as a collaborator. Here, the two perform many of Jerome Kern's most beloved songs including "They Didn't Believe Me," "The Song Is You," "Look for the Silver Lining," "All the Things You Are," and "The Way You Look Tonight."

MICHAEL BUBLÉ

Michael Bublé (February 2003), album, Reprise. In his debut album, Michael Bublé includes standards from the American Songbook such as "The Way You Look Tonight" and "Come Fly with Me" along with what might be called modern classics—songs that have much the same cultural currency as standards even though they have retained a link to a particular performer, such as "Moondance" (originally performed by Van Morrison) and "Fever" (made popular by Peggy Lee). Here, Bublé performs all of these songs with the same musical palette, one that is rooted in the history of the standard even more than his repertoire. He is a crooner through and through, and he is accompanied by a swing band.

Call Me Irresponsible (May 2007), album, Reprise. This album continues to feature a combination of established standard and modern classics, along with a few original additions. He performs standards such as the title track, "The Best Is Yet to Come," "I've Got the World on a String," and "Dream." He reinvents hits like Eric Clapton's "Wonderful Tonight" and Willie Nelson's "Always on My Mind." And he offers his own abilities as lyricist in "Everything."

Crazy Love (October 2009), album, Reprise. This effort from Bublé includes standards such as Arthur Hamilton's "Cry Me a River," Hoagy Carmichael's "Georgia on My Mind" and "Stardust," and the Arthur Freed/Nacio Herb Brown title "All I Do Is Dream of You." Alongside these songs, Bublé offers his fresh take on more recent hits such as Billy Vera's "At This Moment" and Don Henley's "Heartache Tonight" as well as his own titles: "Hold On" and "Haven't Met You Yet."

HARRY CONNICK JR.

When Harry Met Sally: Music from the Motion Picture (July 1989), album, SBME Special Mkts. In this classic collection of song performances from the film, Harry Connick reintroduces the standard and its connection to jazz. Included here are "It Had to Be You," "Love Is Here to Stay," "But Not for Me," "Don't Get Around Much Anymore," "Autumn in New York," and "Let's Call the Whole Thing Off."

Your Songs (September 2009), album, Sony. Representative of Connick more generally, this album includes a number of favorites from the American Songbook as well as a few more recently popularized selections. Harry Connick offers his interpretations of "All the Way," "The Way You Look Tonight," and "Smile" alongside modern classics such as Billy Joel's "Just the Way You Are" and the Elvis Presley hit "Can't Help Falling in Love."

MILES DAVIS

Seven Steps: The Complete Columbia Recordings of Miles Davis 1963–1964 (September 2004), seven-CD set, Columbia. Although the American Songbook as a whole played a relatively small part in Davis's career, individual songs like "My Funny Valentine" and "Autumn Leaves" became an integral part of his repertoire. More importantly, his interpretations of these and other standards provide especially good examples of how the standard remained an important part of jazz in the latter half of the twentieth century—even for innovative and progressive artists like Davis.

DUKE ELLINGTON

Ella Fitzgerald Sings the Duke Ellington Songbook (1957), album, Verve. Here, Ella Fitzgerald not only sings the songs of Duke Ellington; she also collaborates with him and his legendary ensemble. Together, they offer their collaborative renditions of "Caravan," "Mood Indigo," "Satin Doll," "Don't Get Around Much Anymore," "Sophisticated Lady," and, of course, "It Don't Mean a Thing If It Ain't Got That Swing."

The Essential Duke Ellington (June 2005), two-CD set, Sony. This collection offers a solid overview of Ellington as both composer and bandleader. Listeners can hear his original instrumental versions of songs like "Mood Indigo," "In a Sentimental Mood," "Satin Doll," and "It Don't Mean a Thing If It Ain't Got That Swing."

ELLA FITZGERALD

Ella Fitzgerald Sings the Cole Porter Songbook (1956), album, Verve. This is the first of Ella Fitzgerald's songbook albums, something she began when she started recording with the Verve label in 1956. This one includes such Cole Porter favorites as "Anything Goes," "I Get a Kick Out of You," "I Love Paris," "I've Got You Under My Skin," "So in Love," "Night and Day," and "You'd Be So Easy to Love."

Ella Fitzgerald Sings the Rodgers and Hart Songbook (1956), album, Verve. This comprehensive songbook collection includes thirty-six song performances from Fitzgerald, including "This Can't Be Love," "The Lady Is a Tramp," "Thou Swell," "My Funny Valentine," and "Isn't It Romantic."

Ella Fitzgerald Sings the Duke Ellington Songbook (1957), album, Verve. It is hardly surprising that Ella Fitzgerald would team up with the composer and his legendary ensemble for this collection. Together, they offer their collaborative renditions of "Caravan," "Mood Indigo," "Satin Doll," "Don't Get Around Much Anymore," "Sophisticated Lady," and, of course, "It Don't Mean a Thing If It Ain't Got That Swing."

Ella Fitzgerald Sings the Irving Berlin Songbook (1958), album, Verve. This album brings together the full range of Berlin's output. It includes dance-oriented songs such as "Let's Face the Music and Dance," "Cheek to Cheek," and "Puttin' on the Ritz" alongside ballads like "How Deep Is the Ocean?" and "Always," as well as novelty numbers such as "I've Got My Love to Keep Me Warm" and "Isn't This a Lovely Day." It even contains Fitzgerald's rendition of Berlin's "Supper Time," an unusually dark song written from the perspective of a woman whose husband has recently been killed.

Ella Fitzgerald Sings the George and Ira Gershwin Songbook (1959), album Verve. Ella Fitzgerald partnered with renowned orchestrator Nelson Riddle for this collection of Gershwin tunes. Riddle also worked with Frank Sinatra, making him a key figure in the way people were hearing the American Songbook by the 1950s. As in her other composer collections, Fitzgerald's coverage of the Gershwin catalog is extensive. In addition to expected songs like "Let's Call the Whole Thing Off," "I Got Rhythm," "Fascinating Rhythm," and "Oh, Lady Be Good," Fitzgerald includes less familiar tunes from the Gershwin brothers such as "Sam and Delilah," "Just Another Rhumba," and "Somebody from Somewhere."

Ella Fitzgerald Sings the Harold Arlen Songbook (1961), album, Verve. In her compilation of songs from Harold Arlen, Fitzgerald also showcases the work of the major lyricists with whom he collaborated, including Johnny Mercer ("Blues in the Night," "Come Rain or Come Shine"), Ted Koehler ("Stormy Weather," "I've Got the World on a String"), E. Y. Harburg ("Over the Rainbow"), and Ira Gershwin ("The Man That Got Away").

Ella Fitzgerald Sings the Jerome Kern Songbook (1963), album, Verve. Here again, Fitzgerald's collection of Jerome Kern's music also highlights the work of his wordsmith collaborators. In this case, that includes Dorothy Fields ("The Way You Look Tonight," "A Fine Romance") and Oscar Hammerstein ("Can't Help Lovin' Dat Man," "All the Things You Are."). It also reunited her with Nelson Riddle and his orchestra.

Ella Fitzgerald Sings the Johnny Mercer Songbook (1964), album, Verve. For her final songbook compilation, Fitzgerald chose a songwriter who worked primarily as a lyricist rather than a composer—though she includes a couple of selections for which Mercer also contributed music, such as "Dream." This provides a glimpse into the range of talents with whom Mercer worked over the course of his career, including his work with lesser-known songwriters like David Raskin ("Laura") and Richard A. Whiting ("Too Marvelous for Words").

HELEN FORREST

I Had the Craziest Dream: The Golden Years of Helen Forrest (September 2003), four-CD set, Jasmine Music. This collection is a testament to Forrest's understated role in perpetuating the American Songbook. It includes favorites such as "It Had to Be You," "Come Rain or Come Shine," "All of Me," "Skylark," "Smoke Get in Your Eyes," and many more. Her performances here are clear and straightforward, which offered mainstream listeners of the 1930s and 1940s just what they wanted to hear—the songs themselves. This approach may also explain why she has been eclipsed in popular memory by singers with more nuance and individuality, however.

JUDY GARLAND

Judy (1956), album, Capitol. Garland recorded a number of standards as singles in the 1930s and 1940s—before LP albums became the norm in the recording industry. Here, she offers a collection of standards, including "Come Rain or Come Shine," "I Feel a Song Coming On," and "Any Place I Hang My Hat Is Home."

Judy Garland: The Complete Decca Masters (July 1994), four-CD set, Geffen. This compilation offers listeners an easy way to hear the wealth of single records Judy Garland made for the Decca label in the early years of her career. This includes a number of standards she helped introduce such as "Over the Rainbow," "Embraceable You," "That Old Black Magic," "On the Sunny Side of the Street," and "I'm Always Chasing Rainbows."

COLEMAN HAWKINS

Body and Soul: Original Recordings, 1933–1949 (June 2001), album, Naxos. This compilation contains a set of original recordings from saxophonist Coleman Hawkins. His celebrated 1939 rendition of "Body and Soul" is here alongside other standards such as "Night and Day," "I Only Have Eyes for You," "How Deep Is the Ocean," and "Honeysuckle Rose."

BILLIE HOLIDAY

Billie Holiday: Body and Soul (January 1957), album, Verve Records. This album features Holiday's celebrated later rendition of "Body and Soul" as well as beautiful performances of "They Can't Take That Away from Me," "Let's Call the Whole Thing Off," "Gee Baby, Ain't I Good to You," and "Embraceable You." In all of these selections and more, it offers listeners a window into Holiday in her later career, a period characterized by a deteriorating yet often more powerful voice and even more interpretive depth from this beloved singer.

Billie Holiday: Lady in Satin (June 1958), album, Columbia Records. This landmark album from late in Holiday's career features some less widely recorded but no less memorable standards such as the Rodgers and Hart ballad "It's Easy to Remember," the J. Fred Coots and Sam M. Lewis classic "For All We Know," and the Hoagy Carmichael gem "I Get Along Without You Very Well." It also includes her rendition of "I'm a Fool to Want You," a song attributed in part to another celebrated singer of the American Songbook—Frank Sinatra.

Lady Day: The Complete Billie Holiday on Columbia—1933–1944, (June 2012), ten-CD set, Sony Legacy. Holiday's broad coverage of the American Songbook in the first half of her career is readily apparent in this digital compilation. Tunes from the Gershwins, Cole Porter, Irving Berlin, Harry Warren, and more are well represented, as well as her first recording of Johnny Green's "Body and Soul." It even includes multiple takes of some selections, offering listeners the opportunity to experience Holiday's range as an interpreter.

DIANA KRALL

Stepping Out (February 2000), remastered album, Justin Time. This debut album from Diana Krall was released in 1993. It includes her performances of songs such as "This Can't Be Love," "42nd Street," and the iconic jazz standard "Body and Soul." It serves as a well-rounded introduction to her rich, low voice and the unique way she uses it.

The Look of Love (September 2001), album, Verve. In this album, Krall interprets such favorites as "S'Wonderful," "Cry Me a River," and "I Get Along Without You Very Well" along with a few more recent selections like the title track written by Burt Bacharach. She continues to demonstrate a seamless blend of contemporary jazz sensibility and traditional musical material that is quite compelling.

From This Moment On (September 2006), album, Verve. Diana Krall's knowledge and coverage of the American Songbook are deep enough to include songs beyond what listeners might expect, and this is especially true here. She sings a number of lesser-known selections from the most celebrated songwriters, including "I Was Doing All Right" from George and Ira Gershwin, "From This Moment On" from Cole Porter, and "Little Girl Blue" from Richard Rodgers and Lorenz Hart. As always, her renditions also depart from the norm without being overly experimental.

Quiet Nights (March 2009), album, Verve. Beyond another glimpse into the uniqueness of Diana Krall's voice, this album is noteworthy for two things: a tinge of Latin jazz influence and a more eclectic mix of music overall. Along with American Songbook staples such as "Where or When" and "Too Marvelous for Words," we hear several tunes from Brazilian songwriters like Jobim and Marco Valle, "Walk On By" by Burt Bacharach, and "How Can You Mend a Broken Heart" from the Bee Gees.

AUDRA MCDONALD

How Glory Goes (February 2000), album, Nonesuch. This album features a provocative blend of familiar standards and contemporary Broadway selections. From the American Songbook, McDonald chooses mostly songs from Harold Arlen, including "Any Place I Hang My Hat Is Home" and "I Had Myself a True Love" (lyrics by Johnny Mercer) and "The Man That Got Away" (lyrics by Ira Gershwin). Among her contemporary offerings are "Come Down from the Tree" (music by Stephen Flaherty, lyrics by Lynn Ahrens) and the title track, "How Glory Goes" (music and lyrics by Adam Guettel).

ETHEL MERMAN

Ethel Merman: American Music Icon (July 2003), album, American Legends. This compilation offers a solid representation of Ethel Merman's best-known recordings. It includes key songs from the composers who wrote for her onstage—most notably Irving Berlin, George Gershwin, and Cole Porter.

BRIAN STOKES MITCHELL

Brian Stokes Mitchell (June 2006), album, Legacy. This album features adventurous interpretations of several popular standards and some more recent Broadway favorites. Highlights include "The Best Is Yet to Come," "Just in Time," "How Long Has This Been Going On?" and Mitchell's unique blend of Duke Ellington's "Take the 'A' Train" and Stephen Sondheim's "Another Hundred People."

DJANGO REINHARDT

Django Reinhardt and Stephane Grappelli with the Quintet of the Hot Club of France: The Ultimate Collection (January 2009), two-CD set, Not Now. This set offers a comprehensive hearing of the celebrated quintet led by Django Reinhardt and Stephane Grappelli. It includes their interpretation of Duke Ellington's "It Don't Mean a Thing If It Ain't Got That Swing" as well as other familiar standards such as "Jeepers Creepers," "Night and Day," and "Honeysuckle Rose."

The Essential Django Reinhardt (March 2011), two-CD set, Sony Legacy. This collection demonstrates Django Reinhardt's attention to the American Songbook over the course of his life. It includes, for example, his renditions of "Stormy Weather," "I Got Rhythm," "It's Only a Paper Moon," and "All the Things You Are."

ARTIE SHAW

The Essential Artie Shaw (August 2005), two-CD set, RCA. This album showcases the role of standards in the repertoire of major swing bands in the 1930s and 1940s. Artie Shaw was one of many bandleaders whose playlist looked something like the track listing seen here, with the American Songbook constituting about half of the total number of songs. It also includes recordings featuring singers such as Helen Forrest ("All the Things You Are," "Deep in a Dream"), Billie Holiday ("Any Old Time"), and Lena Horne ("Don't Take Your Love from Me").

FRANK SINATRA

The Voice of Sinatra (March 1946), album, Columbia. This album was Frank Sinatra's first, and it sets the tone for most of what followed in Sinatra's career—especially with respect to the repertoire of standards he selected. Originally issued as a set of 78 records, it contained eight songs. Sinatra recorded a number of others at the same time, however, which have since been reissued along with the original eight. This more comprehensive collection of songs shows both broad and deep coverage of the American Songbook, with tunes from big names like Cole Porter and George Gershwin as well as familiar but lesser-known figures like J. Fred Coots, Nacio Herb Brown, and Fred E. Ahlert.

Songs for Young Lovers (1954), album, Capitol. This album marks Sinatra's first work for Capitol Records and his first collaboration with orchestrator Nelson Riddle—both of which proved influential in his career as a whole. Here, Sinatra continues his coverage of the standard catalog. Highlights include "My Funny Valentine," "A Foggy Day," "I Get a Kick Out of You," and "They Can't Take That Away from Me."

Ring-a-Ding Ding! (March 1961), album, Reprise. This album, which marks Sinatra's debut with the Reprise label, features a title track written by standard songwriters Sammy Cahn and Jimmy van Heusen specifically for Sinatra. In addition, he offers reinterpretations of many of his established favorites from the Gershwins, Cole Porter, Irving Berlin, Jerome Kern, and Harold Arlen.

Sinatra-Basie: An Historic Musical First (December 1962), album, Reprise. This album—also cited above under Count Basie—brings together two of the greatest musical talents associated with the American Songbook. Sinatra's previous hits figure prominently, with recordings of "Pennies from Heaven," "The Tender Trap," "Nice Work If You Can Get It," and "Learnin' the Blues."

Ultimate Sinatra (April 2015), four-CD set, Capitol. This compilation offers listeners a comprehensive overview of Sinatra's recorded output, from his early years with Columbia as well as his later work with Capitol and Reprise. Sinatra's extensive coverage of the American Songbook is readily apparent here, with songs like "I Get a Kick Out of You," "In the Wee Small Hours of the Morning," "Stardust," and many more.

INDEX

42nd Street (film), 41–42

AABA song form, 2, 4, 6, 9, 10
"A Pretty Girl Is Like a Melody", 35–36
African American Music, xxiv, xxviii, 3, 51.
 See also jazz
Ahrens, Lynn, 96–97
"Alexander's Ragtime Band", xxviii–xxix
"All the Things You Are", 8–9
An American in Paris (film), 16
animated film, popular songs in, 90,
 104–106
"Anything Goes", 20
April in Paris (film), 53, 56–58
Arlen, Harold, 15–16
Astaire, Fred, 33–34, 39, 41, 42–44,
 68–69, 72, 73, 79

Basie, Count, 57
belting (singing style), 67
Bennett, Tony, xxii, 75–76, 79, 93,
 108–111
Berkeley, Busby, 41
Berlin, Irving, 4–5, 20–23, 35–36, 42, 68
"Blue Skies", 4–5, 11, 39
"Body and Soul", 53, 58–59, 103–104
Bolton, Guy, 31, 34
Breakfast at Tiffany's (film), 47
Broadway, history of, 27–38, 83, 86–89
Brown, Nacio Herb, 44–45
Brown, Jason Robert, 96

Bublé, Michael, xxi, 79, 100–102
Buck, Gene, 28–29

Carmichael, Hoagy, 23–24
Charlap, Bill, 110
Coleman, Cy, 9–11, 88
"Come Down From the Tree", 96
Connick, Harry, Jr., 77, 106–107, 108
Crazy for You (stage production), 16
crooning (singing style), 74

Daniels, Bebe, 41–42
Dubin, Al, 41–42
Duke, Vernon, 56–58

"Easter Parade", 21–22
Ebb, Fred, 88
Ellington, Duke, 53–56, 60

"Fascinating Rhythm", 34
Fields, Dorothy, 43–44, 88
film musical, 39–46, 83, 89. *See also*
 Hollywood, history of
Fitzgerald, Ella, 57, 73–74, 77, 80
Flaherty, Stephen, 96–97
Forever Young (film), 49–50
Forget Paris (film), 57
Forrest, Helen, 69–70, 71, 73
Foster, Stephen, xxiii–xxiv, 27
Freed, Arthur, 44–45, 89

Garland, Judy, 63, 72–73
Gershwin, George and Ira, 6–7, 11, 16, 33–34, 51, 56, 67, 92
Grappelli, Stephane, 54–55, 60
Green, Johnny, 58–59

Hammerstein, Oscar II, 37, 87
Harburg, E. Y., 15–16, 57–58
Hart, Lorenz, 25
Hawkins, Coleman, 58–59
Hello, Dolly! (film), 105, 106
Herman, Jerry, 105–106
Holiday, Billie, 49–50, 59, 70–72, 73, 78
Hollywood, history of, 39–46, 83, 89, 104–106

"I Got Rhythm", 6–7, 11, 16, 92
"Isn't It Romantic", 25
"Isn't This a Lovely Day (To Be Caught in the Rain)", 42
"It Don't Mean a Thing (If It Ain't Got That Swing)", 53–56
"It Had to Be You", 18–19
"It Only Takes a Moment", 105–106

jazz, 51–60, 84, 91–92
Jewish Music, xxiv–xxv

Kander, John, 88
Kelly, Gene, 45–46
Kern, Jerome, 28–33, 37, 43–44, 55
Krall, Diana, 78, 106, 107–108

Lady, Be Good (stage production), 33–35
Lady Gaga, 110
Leigh, Carolyn, 9–11
"Little Jazz Bird", 34
"Look for the Silver Lining", 31–32, 39

Mancini, Henry, 47
McDonald, Audra, 96–100
Mercer, Johnny, xxv, 24, 46–47
Merman, Ethel, 63, 67–68, 73
Miller, Marilyn, 31–33
Mitchell, Brian Stokes, 96–100
Moon River (film), 47
Music Box Revues (stage productions), 36
musical comedy, 30–35, 37–38. *See also* Broadway, history of

musical film. *See* film musical
musical theater. *See* Broadway, history of
My Best Friend's Wedding (film), 48
"My Lady of the Nile", 28

Newman, Thomas, 106
"Night and Day", 7–8

Oklahoma! (stage production), 87
"Over the Rainbow", 15–16

Parish, Mitchell, 23–24
Porter, Cole, xxv, 7–8, 19

Ragtime (stage production), 96–97
recorded music, xxvi–xxviii, 49–50, 63–66, 85, 90
Reinhardt, Django, 54–55
revue, 28–30, 36. *See also* Broadway, history of
rock and roll, 83, 84
Rodgers, Richard, 25, 37–38, 87
Rogers, Ginger, 39, 42–44

Sally (stage production), 31, 33
Show Boat (stage production), 37
Sinatra, Frank, 74–76, 79
Singin' in the Rain (film), 44–46
"Singin' in the Rain", 44–46
"Skylark", 24
Sondheim, Stephen, 88
Spaulding, Esperanza, 103–104
"Stardust", 23–24
Swing! (stage production), 55
Swing Time (film), 43–44

"The Best Is Yet to Come", 9–11
"The Stars and the Moon", 96
"The Very Thought of You", 49–50
"The Way You Look Tonight", 43–44, 48
"They Didn't Believe Me", 28–29
'Till the Clouds Roll By", 31–32

WALL-E (film), 104–106
Warren, Harry, 41–42
"White Christmas", 21, 22
World War I, xxiii, 55
"Wonderful Tonight", 102

"You're Getting to be a Habit With Me", 41–42

"You're the Top", 19–20

Ziegfeld, Florenz, 33

Ziegfeld Follies (stage productions), 28–30, 35–36

ABOUT THE AUTHOR

Ann van der Merwe holds a bachelor's of music in voice performance from the University of Illinois at Urbana-Champaign, where she was awarded the Thomas J. Smith Scholarship in music performance. After graduating summa cum laude, she performed in the national tour of *Anything Goes* and worked at regional theaters in Illinois and Florida.

She then earned MA and PhD degrees in historical musicology from The Ohio State University, where she began her research on American musical theater and popular music. After completing her doctoral studies, she expanded her dissertation research into her first book, *The Ziegfeld Follies: A History in Song* (Scarecrow Press, 2009). She also served on the faculty at Miami University for three years, where she taught a wide variety of courses in music history and appreciation.

She is currently serving as director of children's ministry at Lebanon Presbyterian Church in Lebanon, Ohio, where she is able to pursue all her passions at the same time. She lives with her husband and two adorable children in southwest Ohio.